THE PATH TO EARLY MATH
What Preschool Teachers Need to Know

by Ingrid Crowther, EdD

www.gryphonhouse.com

© 2021 Ingrid Crowther

Published by GRYPHON House, Inc.

P. O. Box 10, Lewisville, NC 27023

800.638.0928; 877.638.7576 [fax]

Visit us on the web at www.gryphonhouse.com.

All rights reserved. No part of this publication may be reproduced or transmitted in any form or by any means, electronic or technical, including photocopy, recording, or any information storage or retrieval system, without prior written permission of the publisher. Printed in the United States. Every effort has been made to locate copyright and permission information.

Cover images used under license from Shutterstock.com and courtesy of the author.

Library of Congress Control Number: 2021934999

Bulk Purchase

Gryphon House books are available for special premiums and sales promotions as well as for fund-raising use. Special editions or book excerpts also can be created to specifications. For details, call 800.638.0928.

Disclaimer

Gryphon House, Inc., cannot be held responsible for damage, mishap, or injury incurred during the use of or because of activities in this book. Appropriate and reasonable caution and adult supervision of children involved in activities and corresponding to the age and capability of each child involved are recommended at all times. Do not leave children unattended at any time. Observe safety and caution at all times.

TABLE OF CONTENTS

Acknowledgments iv

Introduction 1

Chapter 1: Understanding Developing Math Concepts 4

Chapter 2: The Role of the Facilitator: Supportive Environments, Interaction, and Documentation 24

Chapter 3: One-to-One Correspondence 40

Chapter 4: Forming Sets 78

Chapter 5: Object Counting 102

Chapter 6: Patterning 146

Chapter 7: Measurement 174

Chapter 8: Two- and Three-Dimensional Geometric Shapes 200

Chapter 9: Parts and Wholes: Beginning Understanding of Fractions 226

Chapter 10: Computation: Addition and Subtraction 246

References and Recommended Reading 272

Index 275

ACKNOWLEDGMENTS

I would like to acknowledge the participation of the children and families in urban, rural, and isolated settings in child-care programs across Canada (Alberta, British Columbia, Manitoba, Ontario, Yukon, Nunavut, and Prince Edward Island) and from various countries around the world. In particular, I would like to acknowledge Progressive Academy in Edmonton, Alberta, and the Canadian International School, Lakeside Campus, in Singapore for their support. Without the children's interactions and the help of the program staffs, this text would not have been possible.

INTRODUCTION

A variety of books have been published in the area of math, but most of these deal with instruction for school-aged children. According to international research, there is an overwhelming need to focus on appropriate early math development. Most early childhood educators have received very little formal training in math for the early years. Math is a strong predictor of future academic success and is therefore critical to providing strong, firm foundations to young children that lead to lifelong learning. This book attempts to bridge that gap.

Philosophy of This Book

Young children's learning is based on interactions with the important people in their lives: other children, families, early childhood educators, and community members. Math learning, too, begins with the child. Adults build on each child's interests, experiences, and abilities to create appropriate learning environments that function as a third teacher. All parts of the learning environment—home, indoor, outdoor—are equally important. Children's learning depends on their background experiences, which provide opportunities for increased motivation, transfer of skills and abilities from one setting to another, and maximized learning.

Children's environments need to be rich in language. Adults can support language acquisition by providing realistic vocabulary that leads to future understanding of concepts. Therefore, this book has a distinct focus on language acquisition and enhancement. Children love to explore and learn to use the language associated with their explorations. They need to hear language to form the connections between the words and the concepts that they are exploring.

Often adults oversimplify the language they use with children, a practice that deprives them of the richness of spoken language within contexts. It has been said that children taste words. I have certainly witnessed this. Christopher, a two-year-old, loved big words. When he heard a word he liked, he would say it over and over again and finally tried using it in context. For example, he loved the word *annoyed*. On a visit to a store with his mother, he was asked not to touch things but just look. He turned to his mother and asked, "Will the clerk get annoyed?"

The teacher's role is to document learning, coordinate children's activities, interact with families, and ensure that children are engaged as protagonists in active play activities. Additionally, with the increased diversity within most child-care programs, teachers can gain knowledge of ethnic and cultural groups within the child-care community and establish partnerships with families.

Teachers can then embrace and represent various cultural elements to create an environment rich in materials, resources, and experiences.

Organization of the Book

The chapters follow a developmental order. Chapter one sets the stage with an overview of pertinent common concepts for all chapters. The beginning of each chapter provides the learning outcomes for that chapter, followed by a concise definition of the concepts covered and the ages and stages of development related to the skills discussed in the chapter. Each chapter includes specific descriptions of how to set up an appropriate learning environment and how to support interactions and activities within that environment. Student activities at the end of each chapter provide opportunities for independent study or group discussion during class times.

The key concepts in this text are based on children's real experiences, and the theory, methodology, and strategies are integrated with these experiences in mind. Photographs of children engaged in activities that demonstrate specific math concepts and written scenarios to illustrate the activities will support your understanding of how to implement the approaches in your classroom. Each activity includes a description of how to set up appropriate learning environments, including a materials list and additional resources that are relevant to a specific concept area, as well as a series of applied learning exercises and a glossary of terms.

Ways to Use This Book

You may be a teacher who is looking for ways to strengthen the math learning in his early childhood classroom. You may be part of a community of practice, a group of educators who want to learn more about teaching math in developmentally appropriate ways. You may be an educator in a community college or other teacher-training program who wants to offer her students an easy-to-use reference and guide for helping young children develop their math competencies and skills. Irrespective of who you are or what philosophy you follow, this text will help you to hone your skills and abilities to make math learning a fun and worthwhile activity in your setting.

CHAPTER 01

Understanding Developing Math Concepts

"Mathematical thinking is cognitively foundational, and children's early knowledge of math strongly predicts their later success in math."

—Clements and Sarama, "Math in the Early Years: A Strong Predictor for Later School Success"

Across the world, parents, citizens, departments of education, and governments are concerned about the poor math competence of children in the educational systems. "[T]he current situation of more than 20 percent of young Europeans not reaching a minimum level of basic skills in mathematics and science is alarming" (European Commission Directorate-General for Education and Culture, 2013).

In North America, concern has mounted that children's math abilities are decreasing. Many school boards and politicians are looking at ways to improve math instruction in the educational systems. "Math has become a flashpoint in many parts of the country as falling test scores have ignited debate about how the subject is being taught in schools" (Alphonso, 2018). "Over the past decade, there has been no progress in either mathematics or reading performance, and the lowest-performing students are doing worse" (Carr, as quoted in Camera, 2019). Debates have arisen on how to improve math skills, especially for young children.

Math: A Predictor of Future Academic Success

Much research has focused on developing literacy in reading as a predictor of later school success. Research is now beginning to show, however, that early math development is one of the most consistent predictors of later academic performance. A study conducted by Greg J. Duncan and colleagues (2007) found that children's understanding of early math concepts such as knowledge of numbers and ordinality—first, second, third, and so on—are the most powerful predictors of later learning. Similarly, in a report for the Education Commission of the States, researchers Douglas Clements and Julie Sarama (2013) conclude that preschool math also predicts later reading achievement and oral language abilities, including vocabulary competence, making inferences, independent reading activities, and using grammatical complexities. "Given the importance of mathematics to academic success in all subjects, all children need a robust knowledge of mathematics in their earliest years."

Math is a consistent predictor of future success. Many of the core math skills are also foundational to other learning competencies. Math skills encourage active problem solving.

When engaged in appropriate math experiences, children learn to think both convergently and divergently. *Convergent thinking* involves problem solving to arrive at one correct response. *Divergent thinking*, on the other hand, involves using multiple strategies to solve a problem, which may result in a variety of correct responses.

- Math enhances language development.
- Math reinforces expectations for writing and documentation.
- Math supports the development of spatial awareness.
- Math supports the development of matching and sorting skills.
- Math supports the development of patterning skills.

Core math skills transfer to other curricular areas. For example, *one-to-one correspondence* is the concept that numbers have only one possible correct placement. The number 2 will always belong between 1 and 3. This leads to the ability to count objects by:

- matching each object counted to a corresponding verbal number,
- matching a number of objects to a printed or concrete number, and
- recognizing that each number represents a specific quantity.

So, when counting a group of items, each item must be counted only once. Similarly, in reading and writing, each letter in a given word must be in a specific location. For example, in the word *cat*, the letter *a* must be in the middle of the word to spell *cat*. In science, when measuring length, only one number will indicate the appropriate length. In music, only one key on the piano represents middle C. In geography, only one place on the map designates a certain lake.

A *pattern* is a continuous sequence of repeating elements. Poetry, rhymes, and song lyrics are often written with patterns of repeating elements. In science, it is easy to find patterns in nature. For example, plants sprout leaves or petals in repeating arrangements. Seasons come and go in a pattern: winter, spring, summer, and autumn. Plants and animals grow in cycles of repeating stages. Music is usually made up of patterns of notes and rhythms. Art can use patterns of shapes, colors, and lines. In geography, a map can show patterns of streets and other city features.

The math concepts of matching and sorting are also found in other curriculum areas. *Matching* involves finding two items that are the same, such as two red cars. *Sorting* involves grouping more than two items that have the same characteristic, such as red toys or items with wheels. Children can learn to match and sort numbers, letters, and words. They can match two words that end in the same rime (*run* and *bun*) or sort words that begin with the same onset (*run*, *rock*, and *rose*). In science, they can match and sort by color, temperature, texture, and so on. In music, children can match and sort by note pattern or rhythm. Children can match and sort by type of art (painting, sculpture, drawing, and so on) or subject (animals, buildings, flowers, and so on). Geography, too, involves matching and sorting. For example, parks can be located in cities or in rural areas. Cities can be located in different countries, but they are still cities. Two cities can be called by the same name: Springfield, Illinois, and Springfield, Arkansas.

How Children's Thinking Affects Developing Math Concepts

Just as in any other area of human development, acquiring math competencies is a natural progression of learning key concepts and skills that build upon one another. Although core child development in math is universal, children will develop understandings and skills at their own rate, depending on the background experiences of the child. The teacher's knowledge of child development is critical and will help the teacher make decisions about what activities to encourage the children to engage in, what materials to provide, how to organize the environment, and what types of tools to use to document learning. Consider the following aspects of child development.

Concepts and skills develop in a logical sequence; for example, one-to-one correspondence precedes the ability to count objects. Thinking skills develop slowly over time and relate to how children approach tasks and how they solve problems. Since thinking skills are not directly observable, children's interactions with each other and the materials and resources in their learning environments will give clues to what and how they are thinking.

Egocentric Thinking

Egocentric thinking is the first type of thinking that emerges in all children. Children relate everything that happens around them to themselves. At this stage, the child is not yet able to understand a different point of view. What a child sees, hears, tastes, touches, or smells relates to her background experiences and will reflect how she reacts to new situations.

> Melanie, a two-year-old, is very excited to talk to her grandmother on the phone. At one point she exclaims, "Wait a minute!" She runs to her room to get a picture she has painted and holds it up to the phone, which does not have video enabled. Melanie doesn't understand that her grandmother can't see the picture.

> Jeremy, a five-year-old, is getting ready for school one morning. His mother asks him why, and he responds, "It's Monday. I know 'cause I heard it on the news. On Mondays I go to school." His mother explains to him that it is a holiday where they live, but not all over the whole country. Jeremy thinks about it and asks, "Do you mind calling my school and seeing if it is a holiday there too?"

Egocentric thinking disappears gradually with experiences and knowledge, but even adults are sometimes tricked by their perceptions. In a cafeteria at a community college, the large coffee was sold in short, wide cups. Adults were seen pouring their coffee from the shorter cups into tall cups to make sure that they had not been cheated.

Symbolic Thinking

Symbolic thought involves being able to represent ideas in concrete ways. These could include gestures, sounds, actions, words, or creations with objects to represent something other than the objects themselves. As children grow and are exposed to a variety of experiences, they learn to represent their thoughts with words, drawings, songs, music, dance, and dramatic play. In later stages, symbolic thought becomes more abstract, such as solving mathematical problems using equations. Notice the difference in representation of the number five with two different children.

Grace (age four): I made five things on the circles. I used blocks. Each one is different, but see? Each one has five blocks.

Cameron (age five): I like making prints. I made three sets of five prints. I also make five with tallies. My mom uses these to count things fast. Then I made the word and the number and the roman numeral.

Children demonstrate their ability to think and react to situations based on their perceptions. For example, Marlena, a four-year-old, creates equal sets of six objects. She creates them with different objects of different sizes. When she looks at the sets, she appears puzzled. Her teacher notices her expression and asks Marlena what the problem is. Pointing to the snowflakes, Marlena replies, "I counted six, but this one has more. It's longer." She is clearly still confused by what she sees and understands; to her, if items look bigger, that means the set has "more."

In the preschool years, children tend to focus on only one aspect of a situation at a time. This is called *centration*. For example, Brennan, a five-year-old, is creating patterns. He only makes patterns using one variable, however: color. He is unable to extend his patterning to accommodate changes in direction.

Young children are unable to reverse the direction of a particular sequence to go back to the starting point. They may also believe that something that has been done cannot be undone.

> Two four-year-old children are sitting at the snack table, each with one cookie. Oliver breaks his cookie into a number of pieces and laughingly says to Jen, "I have more cookies than you do." Jen promptly bursts into tears, claiming to want more cookies. She does not yet understand that the pieces came from the same size cookie she has.

Children learn as they work with others. Four girls in a kindergarten class are working at the Lego table. Marlena and Eorda have decided to build a town and have divided the board in half with a line of blue Lego blocks. Each girl started to build on her half, but the activity quickly changed to a more collaborative effort over both sections of the board. Faith and Davina

Chapter 1: Understanding Developing Math Concepts

have noticed the activity and want to join them. Since the girls have already started to build, they use a magic marker to divide one of the halves into two quarters. Marlena indicates, "There's four of us and now each of us has one quarter space." Marlena relates her knowledge of fractions to the situation. She does not yet realize that using fractions in any situation requires a division of equal parts.

Children react to external stimuli, and they often get confused when too many stimuli are presented at one time. How a child approaches a task or solves a problem depends on how things are organized.

Six-year-old William is patterning by number (two vehicles each time) and by shape. The container he is using holds only blue vehicles: trains, buses, cars, and boats. He starts out by patterning two buses and two planes. Then he looks into the container and picks up a train and adds it to his pattern. He then switches to patterning by trains and boats. He ends his pattern with two buses. He has been influenced by what he has seen and, therefore, continues with one pattern—number—but changes the shape pattern.

Aaliyah, a five-year-old, has decided to build using a variety of different colored blocks. She explains, "I want to see how high I can make my tower." When she has completed her activity, her teacher, Miranda, asks her how many blocks she has used. As Aaliyah counts, she becomes confused because of the alignment of the blocks and counts some more than once and some not at all. As a result, she is not able to accurately count the number of blocks.

As they grow and develop, children begin to think abstractly. For example, Sarah is a five-year-old who loves to work with numbers. In her spare time, she has created her own number sheet: "All the numbers adding up to twenty that I remember." When asked how she did this, she replies, "Some of them I memorized 'cause I practiced them. Some of the harder ones I just counted in my head."

Reflective Thinking

Reflective thinking is encouraging a child to think about her activities, to think about why she did what she did. Through reflective thinking, children can learn to problem solve.

- What went well? What did not go well?
- How is the activity the same as or different from previous similar activities?
- What has been learned? What still needs to be learned?

Five-year-old Myra has traced around her palm on a piece of paper. Her teacher, Marquita, notices Myra frowning as she looks at her tracing.

Marquita: I notice that you don't look happy. Do you have a problem with what you drew?

Myra: Look at my hand. My fingers are not that fat. They look disgusting. There are only four fingers that I can see.

Marquita: Why do you think that happened?

Myra (shrugging): Maybe I went too fast? No, I think I spread my fingers out too much. I'm going to do it again.

After Myra has finished, she compares the two tracings. "I like this one much better. My fingers are not too fat. It looks more like my hand."

Marquita: What have you learned about tracing your hand?

Myra (thinking): Sometimes I rush too much. I want to do things fast, so I need to slow down. My mom says I rush things too much. I also need to keep my fingers closer together. I guess I need to get better using a pencil. I guess I just have to practice.

Children need guidance through a process to gain reflective thinking skills. The stages of reflective thinking are outlined below (adapted from Crowther, 2018b).

- **Prereflective thinking stage:** In the prereflective stage, children base what they know about the world around them on their personal experiences filtered through the maturation of each child. To understand children's thinking and approaches to learning, consider the knowledge children have gained and observe their actions to see how they use that knowledge. Children need to learn to recognize the following:
    » What they know
    » What they don't know
    » How they can achieve new knowledge

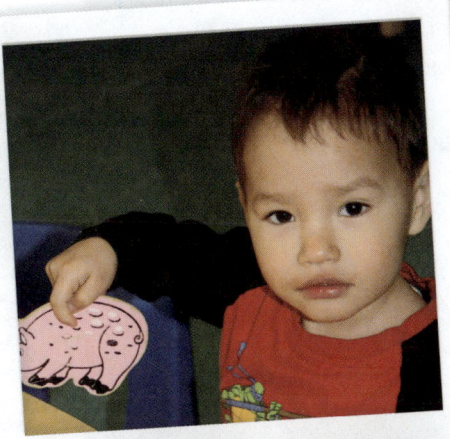

Children in an isolated northern Canadian community have become very interested in farm animals. All their knowledge is based on puzzles and some storybooks about farm animals. Their teachers decide to provide displays of photographs of farm animals for the children to look at and compare. When Jude looks at the photograph of a pig, he shakes his head vigorously and says quite firmly, "Not a pig!" He runs to the puzzle area and brings back the puzzle of a pig and declares, "*This* is a pig!" He cannot be convinced otherwise. Jude is confused by the differing shapes and colors of the two pigs. He also has had no experiences with actual pigs.

Children need sensory experiences with concrete materials to develop how they approach learning. For example, the children in a kindergarten class have decided to build ramps to measure how far their toy cars can travel. They tape a piece of measuring tape to the floor, then try out the different vehicles. Through this hands-on experience, they identify that the bigger cars travel farther.

Young children can become easily frustrated because their understanding is based on absolutes: a concept is either right or wrong. For example, when Keysha finished her drawing of a variety of geometric shapes, she crumpled it up and threw it into the garbage. When her friend Amari asked why she did that, Keysha said, "It was all wrong! The shapes don't look right." Hearing this, her teacher asked her if she wanted to try again. Keysha answered, "No! I can't do it right!"

Young children form opinions and beliefs based not on factual evidence but on what they see and hear around them. So, if the telephone pole in the distance looks shorter, it *is* shorter. If a set of items looks like it has more items, then there *are* more. Young children also form their concepts and beliefs through interactions with authority figures, such as family members and teachers. For example, children in a kindergarten class watched videos of animal movement and became fascinated by speed. Jamie declared that he knew that cheetahs were the fastest animals. When asked how he knew this, he answered, "My dad told me, and he knows everything!"

- **Reflective thinking stage:** At this stage, children continue to consider their knowledge generally absolute, but they begin to justify or look for evidence for what they think. They will engage in activities, such as experimenting, asking questions, or asking for help to look things up on the internet or in books, to justify their answers.

Li Bai, a six-year-old, is measuring how much water is contained in two equal-sized containers, one skinny and tall and one short and wide. He is puzzled because he had thought that the tall one held more water. Li Bai decides to do an "experiment." He uses a measuring cup to measure the amount of water held by each container and graphs each full cup on a graph. He is astonished to find out that each bottle contains the same amount. He tells his teacher, "I'm going to check other stuff so I don't get tricked again."

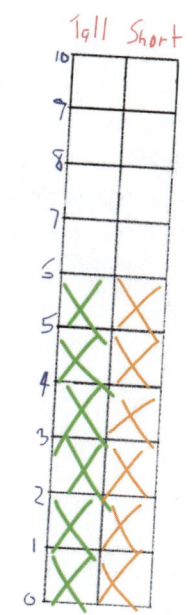

At this stage, children have gained greater language and interaction skills. They actively pursue activities to establish what works and what doesn't, leading them to conclusions about right and wrong. They learn from observing others, listening to ideas expressed, asking and answering questions, and engaging in discussions.

The children in a kindergarten class have been working on forming different sets of numbers with concrete materials, then counting them to identify which have more pieces or fewer pieces. Jayanti has discovered that she can use her sets to develop number stories. Her teacher showed her how to write number stories, and Jayanti has become very enthusiastic about creating her stories. Mara, who has been listening to Jayanti and her teacher, indicates that she has created a number story too. She asks, "Can you show me how to write it, please?"

Chapter 1: Understanding Developing Math Concepts

Although children at his stage still hold beliefs not based on facts, they are increasingly moving toward looking for facts to support reasoning. They will use manipulative materials, for example, to gain understanding about addition and subtraction. As they continue to form concepts and beliefs, children will look toward personal heroes and friends as well as authority figures. In conflicting situations, a child may well pick one authority over another. For example, Jeremiah, a six-year-old, is learning about place value at school. At home, he shows his parents how he learned about place values using a hundred chart. His father says he could show Jeremiah a different way to do this, but Jeremiah prefers to use the way his teacher has shown him—the "correct" way.

How Children's Developing Fine-Motor Control Affects Math Learning

Fine-motor development is an important concept to think about and develop in relationship to math concepts. Fine-motor skills provide children with the abilities to successfully do the following:

- Manipulate objects effectively: For example, as children count, they need to touch or move one object at a time to arrive at an accurate count.
- Develop a tripod grasp: A tripod grasp uses the thumb, middle, and index fingers to print or draw, which effectively allows the child to print numbers or draw a specific shape.
- Develop eye-hand coordination to manipulate objects to create sets of different numbers.

Children start to use the tripod grasp, using three or four fingers to hold a writing utensil to print, draw, or write, at about three and a half to four years of age. In the initial stage, the child's fingers do not move independently, and movement is initiated from the wrist. Often, a child will hold the writing tool very tightly, which can lead to muscle strain if this grasp is overused.

Between the ages of four and six years, the dynamic tripod grasp develops. The fingers start to move independently of the wrist, and the grasp is much more relaxed.

Depending on the child's ability to hold and use writing tools effectively, she may struggle to sustain writing effort and to fit numbers or shapes into confined spaces. As a result, children may avoid writing tasks and may develop poor pencil control.

As their control over fine-motor skills increases, they will be able to take advantage of learning through a greater variety of activities. For example, they will be better able to manipulate objects to find answers, such as by forming equal or unequal sets of numbers or by using objects to add to or subtract from a set. They will gain increased independence to do things by themselves, and they will be able to more easily represent what they have created through written documentation.

For example, Jayanti and Mara continued with their activity to create number stories independently. Eventually, they asked their teacher to create a booklet for them so they could share their number stories with their friends.

How Play Influences Math Learning

As children grow and develop, they engage in different types of play. The type of play they engage in is relevant to math development because it predicts how children will interact with each other and how they will most likely interact with the materials in the environment.

Solitary Play

Solitary play, when a child plays by herself, is typically the type of play seen in infants and toddlers, but older children engage in this type of play too. Very young children will investigate objects and what they can do. For example, they will explore textures, tastes, whether or not an object will roll, how an object sounds when it is shaken or dropped, and so on. Through

their explorations, infants will begin to learn about concepts such as one-to-one correspondence, and they will develop vocabulary understanding when they hear an adult describe what they are doing: "I see you put one green bear in the basket." "You put one big bear on the big bridge."

Toddlers will practice their emerging skills as they play by themselves, often talking to themselves as they do. For example, Jordan took the muffin tray from the daily living area to the math area and put one vehicle in each cup. He said to himself, "One red train in this one, and one blue train in this one . . ." With age, children will use solitary play increasingly as a strategy to practice skills, discover new ways of doing, or just work by themselves.

Parallel Play

Parallel play—children playing side by side but not interacting or sharing materials or ideas—appears in the toddler years and continues into preschool. Children this age are learning to play near others. They are interested in what others are doing and will observe other children. They may modify their own activities based on what they observe.

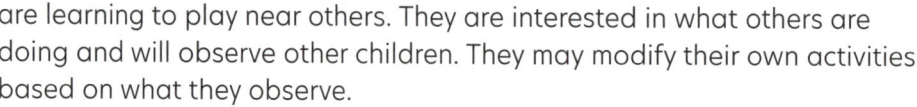

Parker and Naijeer, both three years old, knelt near each other, rolling their toy cars back and forth. Parker watched Naijeer roll his car down a ramp as he said, "Vroo-oo-oom." Parker began rolling her car along the wooden racetrack, saying, "Vroom, vroom."

Older children may engage in parallel activity if they are exploring something new, if they are unsure how to do something, or if they are interested in what someone else is doing.

Associative Play

Preschoolers will begin to engage in *associative play*—play that includes two or more children—as they learn from others through social interactions. They will share ideas and materials but will complete tasks in different ways. They will begin to engage in reflective thinking by sharing their ideas and accomplishments with each other.

> Anna and Roch-John are both creating geometric shapes using small colorful sticks of the same size. The two children share the materials and talk to each other about what they each have created, but they continue to build their own individual structures.
>
> **Anna:** See, I made a hexagon.
>
> **Roch-John:** Cool. I made two shapes: a square and triangle.

Chapter 1: Understanding Developing Math Concepts

Cooperative Play

Cooperative play includes two or more children and involves goal setting, planning, and role assignments. Older preschoolers and school-age children will practice ways to accomplish tasks, learn to coordinate their efforts, and develop the skills needed to work on projects over longer periods of time.

In an activity that lasted for more than two weeks, a group of six-year-old children created a pattern farm. They collected the materials they needed and planned how to create the farm. They used stones and craft sticks of various sizes and colors, along with playdough, to create color or size patterns to make fences. They used paper, scrap cloth pieces, and felt pieces to represent pastures, open areas, ponds, and rivers. They lined up animals in patterns of type or size. The children worked together to create various fields and eventually put them together in a large display of their efforts.

Chapter Summary

The adult's knowledge about children's developmental stages is critical, as it provides a firm process to help to plan and organize the learning environment, activities, materials, and experiences for children in any setting. It ensures that all the children's skills and abilities are met and that the learning environment is set up to encourage maximum participation, growth, and development and to nurture all children as individuals or in group settings.

Apply the Learning

1. Evian and Carlena are often involved in parallel play. What strategies could their teacher use to encourage the two of them to move toward associative play? Consider the use of materials, the learning space, and the adult interactions with the children.

2. Reah, a four-year-old, has created the following drawing. What skills and abilities can you identify in Reah's creation? Consider fine-motor and cognitive skills.

3. Reah is often very critical of her own abilities. You see her crumpling up her work and throwing it in the garbage while she mutters comments such as, "It's no good." What reflective strategies might you engage in to help her see her work more realistically?

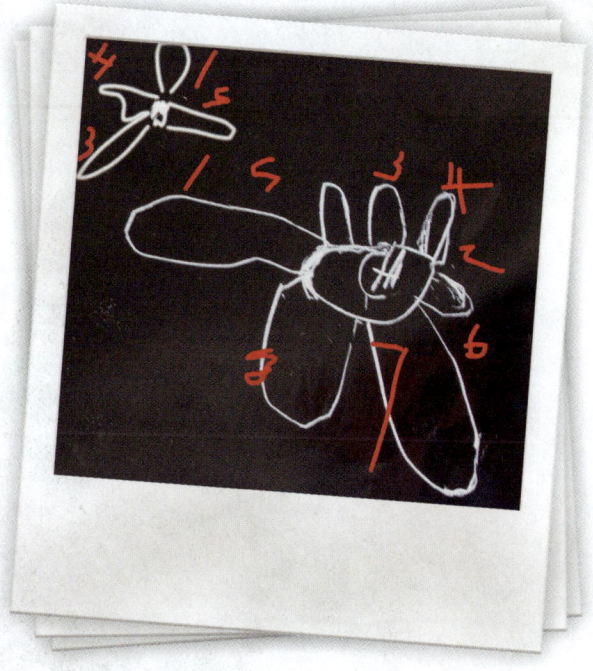

CHAPTER 02

The Role of the Facilitator:
Supportive Environments, Interaction, and Documentation

"Importantly, mathematics teaching and learning needs to become more visual—there is not a single idea or concept that cannot be illustrated or thought about visually."

—Jo Boaler, *Mathematical Mindsets*

The cornerstone of *active learning*—learning by making choices—is encouraging children to initiate their own activities in an environment rich in concrete and realistic experiences. Let children choose where, how, and when to engage, and give them rich materials to choose from that will make their learning visible. Math fits easily in both independent and group activities across the curriculum: drama, science, music, art, manipulatives, reading, carpentry, blocks, water, and sand.

Young children learn best when they can manipulate real objects and be involved in realistic settings. These kinds of strategies ensure that learning is based on children's background experiences. Children learn best when they are in learning environments that represent organization in the real world.

Encourage children to make their thinking visual through the use of blocks, drawings, pictures, playdough, and other open-ended materials, and create settings where they can use their senses to develop their understanding of their experiences.

Provide Organized Spaces

Create an environment that encourages children to make real choices and engage actively with the materials. Provide a variety of materials that represent the interests, skills, and abilities of all the children. Provide an environment that is free of clutter and disorganization. Children will develop an aesthetic appreciation of well-organized spaces and pride in keeping a neat and tidy environment. Make your expectations clear and realistic. Teach them how and give them opportunities to plan for what they will need in their explorations, collect the materials, and take them where they want to work; portable storage is great for this.

Avoid mixing different types of materials in containers. When materials are mixed together, children struggle to find what they are looking for and will often dump out a container's contents. Lack of clear organization limits the room available for creative explorations and distracts children from the learning they can accomplish. It is hard for them to know what to do. Children may start to use materials inappropriately and will leave the dumped materials where they are.

Show the children how to return materials when they have finished their activity. Cleanup time is a great opportunity to practice matching and sorting as they return materials to designated containers and storage locations. Children will develop respect for the materials and learning areas as they recognize that materials are easier to locate in organized spaces.

Table 2.1: Benefits of an Organized Learning Environment

BENEFITS TO CHILDREN	BENEFITS TO ADULTS
• Opportunities to make choices • Increased ability for children to reflect on what they need and want to learn • Decrease in challenging behaviors • Opportunities to solve problems, such as what to work on, where to work, materials to use, and how to transfer learning to new situations • More motivation to clean up after themselves • Increased independence • Less dependence on adults to initiate activities	• Less time spent on setting up individual activities each day • More time to engage children in reflective thinking • More time to focus on individuals or small groups of children • Ability to support activities based on individual strengths, needs, and requests • Less time spent on cleanup

Chapter 2: The Role of the Facilitator

Choosing Materials

Organization reflects an *intentional learning approach*—an approach that is based on the emergent skills (those on the verge of developing) and the behaviors of the children. Children need to practice emergent skills, and not all children are at the same level of skill development. Therefore, reflect on the skills you want to support in the children you work with and the activities that will help them develop those skills. Provide appropriate materials to encourage active participation in the activities. For example, if the purpose of an activity is to encourage patterning, provide materials that offer choices of color, shape, or size, along with patterning strips or materials to encourage patterning.

Provide realistic materials. Often materials used in early childhood settings focus on safety rather than on using familiar, real materials. When children use materials that might break, such as glasses or ceramic plates, they learn to handle materials respectfully, understand the concept of safe handling, and appreciate an aesthetic environment. Of course, you must be careful to follow the safety standards of your program, but provide realistic materials whenever possible.

Provide enough materials to support development of a number of individual skills. For example, if you have observed a child beginning to pattern by color, provide materials that are the same in size and shape, but offer different colors of the materials in each container. When you narrow the choice to color, rather than to shape or size, the child will be able to concentrate on patterning by color.

Maintain interest by providing alternative materials, rotating materials, or supplying new materials to support concept development. Be sure to provide adequate storage so that learning areas do not become cluttered.

Organizing Materials

Spaces in early childhood classrooms are often challenging. There are, however, a number of ways to mitigate overcrowding and still provide adequate space for the numerous activities that young children should engage in.

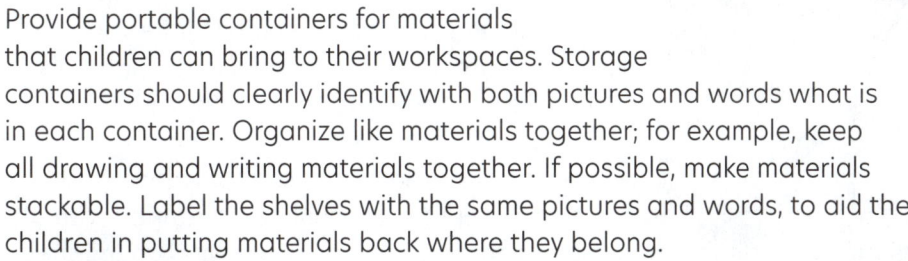

Provide portable containers for materials that children can bring to their workspaces. Storage containers should clearly identify with both pictures and words what is in each container. Organize like materials together; for example, keep all drawing and writing materials together. If possible, make materials stackable. Label the shelves with the same pictures and words, to aid the children in putting materials back where they belong.

Teach the children to return their materials to the appropriate containers and storage areas when they are finished with them. This approach will support children as they learn greater independence. Labels help them find and return materials and also encourage the development of early reading skills.

- **Portable containers with handles:** Children can use baskets, caddies, or small pails to collect needed materials and take them to workspaces.
- **Plastic units with drawers and rollers:** This type of storage can be rolled to any location. These units are suitable for storing accessories that can be used in multiple locations or for storing personal items belonging to the children.
- **Plastic milk crates or filing cartons:** These make good storage containers and can double as extra seating as well. Cover each carton with a wooden lid and a cushion to offer more seating spaces.

- **Open shelves:** These offer easy access to materials. Label each shelf to indicate what belongs there. Labels should have both words and pictures. Providing outlines of items such as blocks can be helpful as well.

Organizing Workspaces and Displays

Use spaces for more than one purpose. For example, create workspaces that children can use for different activities. Organize materials by type in central locations for easy access, and put those materials that share a purpose in common areas. This saves space, as only one area is needed. Provide tables where children can share materials. For example, math materials can be used at a table during free-play activities. The same table can later serve as a snack area or be used for writing and drawing. The room could be arranged with all the materials on labeled shelves around the periphery of the room. Children can plan and choose their materials to take to the tables.

When space is limited, involve the children in helping to decide where unfinished projects can be kept. In one instance, the children decided they could sit around their creation to conduct a group meeting. Another group suggested that they could sit at the tables where the projects were located, but they could turn their chairs around to see everyone. Projects also can be built on a large sheet of plywood that has been sanded smooth to remove splinters. The plywood can then be placed on top of tables or on top of the sand-and-water table until needed. This may mean moving the project several times, but it is worth the effort as children can continue to work on it over time.

Provide displays of the children's finished work. For example, showcase their work on the backs of shelves and on doors and walls. Use booklets to display two-dimensional (2-D) work, and keep the booklets in the common area in file folders where children can easily retrieve them. Create stand-up displays that can be moved from area to area to encourage activity. Display children's three-dimensional (3-D) work on top of shelves, on windowsills, and out in the hall on a table. For large 3-D creations, take photos and collect them in a book or display them in the classroom.

Provide Guidance and Support

The role of the adult in any learning environment is critical and varies along a continuum of two extremes—direct instruction or facilitated instruction. *Direct instruction* is when the adult gives children information on the goal expected and how they are to achieve the task. *Facilitated instruction*, in contrast, means that the adult provides information and sets up the learning environment to encourage children to choose how to actively manipulate or transform materials or experiment in individual ways to expand their learning. Research clearly shows that children need to be actively engaged to maximize their learning. "This is only likely to happen in classrooms that emphasize rich problem solving and the engagement of many approaches to mathematical situations and give attention to and value students' mathematical reasoning" (Small, 2017).

Table 2.2: Direct versus Facilitated Instruction

DIRECT INSTRUCTION	FACILITATED INSTRUCTION
• Adult sets up activities to support specific learning outcomes • Adult is responsible for children's learning • Adult teaches concepts in a group setting • Adult sets rules of behavior and activities • Adult assigns competence • Adult decides when and how long children will engage in activities • Adult decides where the activity will take place • Adult decides how the activity is to be done • Adult is in charge of cleanup	• Adult sets up learning environment to encourage children to make independent choices • Adult and children are jointly responsible for individual learning • Children interact individually or in a group based on common interest, ability, and choice • Adult and children set rules jointly • Children are guided to reflect on personal competence • Children decide when and for how long they will participate in an activity • Children choose where they will engage in activities • Children decide how they will accomplish a task • Children clean up when tasks are completed

Remember that this is a continuum of approaches. At times, teachers and children will use a blended approach. For example, direct instruction helps children learn about safety or gives them background information needed to begin an exploration. A blended approach might be used to time activities, because daily schedules often necessitate that certain events, such as mealtime or outdoor playtime, occur at specific times. Strategies need to be put in place to allow children to continue their individual efforts at another time.

Planning

Planning is a cyclical process. It begins with observing and documenting information about each child. This gives valuable information on his interests, developmental level, skills, and abilities. With this information, the teacher can gather relevant materials based on children's interests, provide activities appropriate to their developmental levels, organize the learning environment to meet their skills and abilities, and engage them in gathering and organizing the learning environment.

Documenting and Assessing Children's Math Abilities

Kate Tarrant, author of *Assessment: Effective Use of Appropriate Assessments in Prekindergarten through 3rd Grade*, reminds us that young children learn and can demonstrate their skills and knowledge in ways that differ significantly from older students. Consequently, "assessment for young children (under age 8) is quite different from the strategies that work with older students" (Tarrant, 2014). There are several reasons for this.

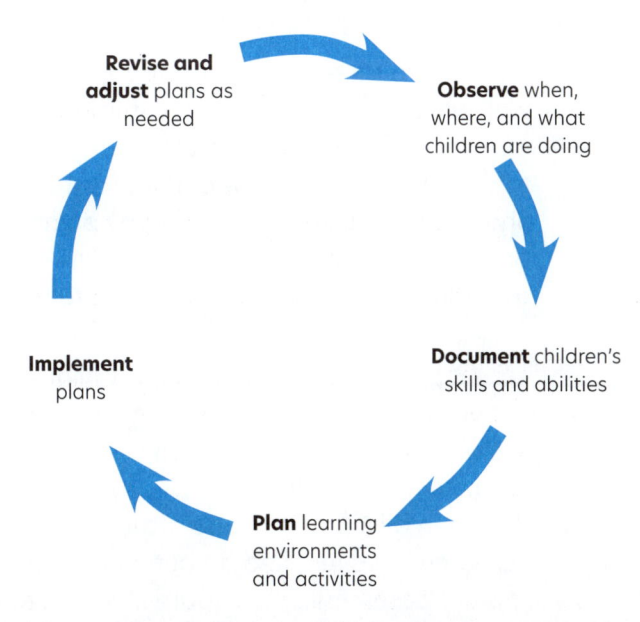

- **Revise and adjust** plans as needed
- **Observe** when, where, and what children are doing
- **Document** children's skills and abilities
- **Plan** learning environments and activities
- **Implement** plans

Children's growth and development in the early years is rapid. As a result, their skills and abilities also change rapidly—sometimes from one day to the next. This means that a skill assessed and not yet learned could be there the next day.

Children's growth patterns are unpredictable. Although many skills and abilities emerge in a predictable order, the growth pattern is individual and may be erratic. Some skills may develop quickly and others at a much slower pace. In many learning environments, educators assess children at specific times, usually before interviews or before developing reports. The timing of an assessment gives only a snapshot of what the child can do on that day at that specific time. Assessments do not consider a child's rapid, ever-changing skills and abilities. As a result, assessment can lead to erroneous assumptions.

Children's skills and abilities are interrelated. Often tests are specific to one skill in isolation, such as counting in math.

> Five-year-old Leona can count objects up to twenty quite well when she is engaged in counting physical objects or actions. But when she is tested using pictures and asked to write the numbers under the pictures, she fails the task. She has been used to counting by pointing to objects or engaging in physical activities. The worksheet-type assessment is not something she is familiar with.

There are two types of general assessment: summative and formative. *Summative assessments* are based on testing skills at a specific time, such as at the end of a unit of study. They evaluate, for example, a child's ability to pattern by more than one attribute; they can also identify whether children have reached an outcome, such as object counting to ten. Summative assessments compare students to each other and provide an evaluative component, such as a comment or a letter or number grade. *Formative assessments*, in contrast, are ongoing evaluations of progress over time. They are used to monitor children individually with the goal to improve learning. They provide teachers with an overview about the strengths and needs of each child. As described above, children's knowledge, skills, and abilities are continually changing at a rapid rate; therefore, using formative assessment in the early years would seem to be the best approach. However, some factors need to be considered for this approach to work:

- The educator must have a firm understanding of child development.
- The learning environment must offer rich resources and materials.
- Children must have opportunities to transfer learning in one situation to other situations.

Administrators and educators need to have a firm understanding of child development. For example, Marlena, four years old, loves to work with numbers. She often forms sets of objects and can count them accurately. However, if sets of equal numbers of objects are aligned so that one appears longer than another, she easily becomes confused. She will indicate one set has more than another set, even after counting each set. Her teacher is puzzled by this fact. She is not aware that Marlena has not yet developed the concept of *conservation of number:* quantities remain constant irrespective of how they are aligned.

To maximize children's free exploration and foster success, the learning environment must be rich in resources and materials. For example, patterning activities provided to children tend to focus on materials that encourage patterning by shape and color. However, children also need to have materials that encourage them to focus on patterning by size and number, and by more than one variable.

Children need to have opportunities to transfer their learning to other situations. This practice not only reinforces the learning but also leads to more divergent thinking and problem solving.

> Ben is sitting outside the kindergarten classroom with his peers, ready to go out to the playground. He suddenly jumps up and exclaims, "Look! We have a pattern: boy, girl, boy, girl! But you have to move!" He points to a peer. The children quickly shift themselves into a boy-girl pattern. Ben declares, "We have a children pattern." When they go outside, Nellie, their teacher, encourages the children to create other patterns, and she photographs them. She plans to print the pictures and let the children pattern with them when they go back inside.

Formative Documentation Strategies

Documenting learning is a very important part of supporting skill development and providing solid foundations for lifelong learning. As new skills emerge, children need to practice them in a variety of settings and at numerous different times. Some research indicates that children may need a minimum of forty repetitions in different settings and over time to gain mastery of new skills (Montessori Academy, 2017). Practice must be deliberate to engage children to pay attention, transfer learning of activities to different settings, set goals, solve problems, and reflect upon what they have learned in order to gain mastery of new skills and abilities (Brabeck, Jeffrey, and Fry, 2010). Emergent skills appear rapidly, but to confirm mastery, a skill must be observed over time to ensure that a child has had adequate practice. Therefore, it is important to observe each skill at least three times and in different settings (Crowther, 2018c).

In each of the following chapters, we will look in detail at various ways to document learning of specific concepts. Some of these strategies include the following:

- Photographs of children's achievements
- Collections of children's works
- Audio or video collections
- Children evaluating themselves using graphs and examples of work

Two important ways of documenting learning are the developmental checklist and the rubric.

- With a *developmental checklist*, the teacher determines whether a child has accomplished a skill by observing him. The teacher then checks the skill off and notes the date of evaluation.
- A *rubric* is a reliable and valid tool to observe and document each child's skills and abilities to provide a clear indication of his progress. A rubric measures skills and abilities in a developmental order using measurable statements that are *reliable* (obtain similar results by all users) and valid (measure what is supposed to be measured). A rubric provides information that gives the educator the next steps for the child to achieve.

Documenting children's progress is most important because it provides the adult with knowledge about an individual child's skills and abilities. Based on this information, activities, experiences, and materials can be provided to engage children's learning. This allows for an individualized approach as well as a group approach. Since information will be available about all the children, it can be used to group children needing the same skill or concept.

Facilitating the Learning

As children engage in activities and explorations, observe them and know when to step in or when to allow them to handle their own problems. Interact positively with children by getting down to their level and expressing interest in what they are doing. Children will often respond to a little reinforcement as they try to work through challenges. Know what type of reinforcement works best with individual children, such as a smile, physical touch, or encouraging positive words. Be responsive and offer additional help as needed. This could involve finding alternative materials that work better, scaffolding the child as he tries to master a task, or helping him identify the problem and consider possible solutions.

Challenging situations can be avoided by paying attention to the children's reactions. Look for signs of stress, frustration, or overexcitement. In these situations, it is important to interact immediately to keep the behaviors from escalating. Be an active listener. Listen to the child's words and observe the intent of the message—expressed both verbally and through body language—without judgment. Clarify the messages you are hearing and observing. Sometimes children have difficulty expressing themselves so that others can understand their intent. In these situations, adults might use the following strategy.

Ms. Jenny noticed that Jesús was showing signs of frustration and that he was starting to shout at the two other children in the large-block area. Jenny got down to the children's level and spoke with them.

JENNY: I noticed that you are getting frustrated, Jesús. Can you say why?

JESÚS: I just think it's not big enough.

JENNY: Why do you think it is not big enough?

JESÚS: There's three, so it's too small.

JENNY: I think I heard you say that there needs to be enough space for three people to fit. Is that correct? (Jesús nodded.)

JENNY [to the other children]: What do you think about Jesús's idea about making a space big enough to fit three people?

The other children thought about it and said that they could work together to make the block structure bigger so that they could all fit.

By using reflective and responsive listening, the teacher is able to encourage the child to express the reason for his frustration and to encourage all three children to find a way to solve the problem.

Chapter Summary

Knowledge of child development is critical. It not only helps in planning an appropriate math curriculum but also helps the teacher support the children's emergent skills. It's never a question of whether a child can do something, but rather whether he *should* be doing it. That implies that the math activities are scaffolded to meet individual skills and abilities to build a strong foundation and love of learning that will continue to grow over time.

Apply the Learning

1. Review your math area, and make a list of the materials already available. Then, organize the materials into math-concept areas. For each math-concept area identify the following:
   - What materials are still needed?
   - How should the materials in each area be organized?
   - Where should each area be set up?

   Implement one math concept area.

2. Observe the children's abilities to count objects.
   - What strategies do the children use?
   - What types of errors do you observe in the children's ability to count?
   - What is the range of object-counting ability in your group?
   - How can you use this information to plan activities to increase each child's ability to count objects?

3. You have a concerned parent who questions why the children engage in play to learn. How can you help the parent understand why play is the best way for young children to learn?

4. Think about or discuss why formative documentation is the best way to evaluate young children's skills and abilities.

5. Identify your personal skill level in encouraging math development for the children you work with.
   - What skills do you already have?
   - What skills do you still need?
   - Identify where you could get the skills you still need.

CHAPTER 03

One-to-One Correspondence

"... one-to-one correspondence of object to object is also necessary before the child can carry out meaningful counting and higher calculations."

—Research and Development Institute, Inc.

One-to-One Correspondence Defined

One-to-one correspondence is one of the core abilities and skills that children need to develop as the basis for building later math concepts, such as counting, patterning, measuring, or solving computation problems. For example, each item in a pattern has a specific place, such as one purple stegosaurus being followed each time by one green stegosaurus.

Items are ordered according to size from largest to smallest or smallest to largest. Each number and symbol in addition, subtraction, division, or multiplication has a regular order, such as 3 + 6 = 9. Children learn to recognize that corners in such geometric shapes as rectangles, squares, or triangles are followed by straight lines and more corners.

The term *one-to-one correspondence* refers to the understanding that only one object occupies a defined space and that, in a set of objects, only one object is identified by a specific number. Children begin to develop one-to-one correspondence skills when they match or place one object next to or on another. For example, on a linear placement mat, Sophie has matched an equal number of orange airplanes to photographs of the planes. She then decides to use buses to match the number of planes by placing one bus under each plane. She excitedly declares, "I have the same number of planes and buses!"

Myra has taken one-to-one correspondence a step further and is demonstrating the skill of counting: recognizing and understanding that each number represents a specific number of objects. Myra places small wooden people on butterflies, matching one person to one butterfly. As she works, she says, "There's one person on each butterfly. Now the butterflies can't fly anymore. There's seven people." With unit blocks, Danny measures the playdough strings he has created to compare which one is the longest.

Ages and Stages of One-to-One Correspondence

Math concepts and skills start to develop early. Infants begin to form ideas about the concept of one-to-one correspondence based on their daily experiences and their interactions with their primary caregivers. Caregivers provide the language to describe the actions and activities the infant engages in. For example, infants may explore and hear language about:

- One sock on one foot
- One spoon of food at a time
- One plate for each person
- One step at a time

Table 3.1: Ages and Stages of One-to-One Correspondence

AGE	SKILL DEVELOPMENT
Infant to two years old	Learns about one-to-one correspondence by listening, observing, and completing tasks such as putting together simple one-piece puzzles or taking off and/or putting on shoes and socks
Two to four years old	Uses one-to-one correspondence strategy to line up objects or place one object on another object; begins to create and compare sets of objects (same, more, fewer) using one-to-one correspondence strategy
Four to five years old	Uses one-to-one correspondence to compare sets of numbers with a greater variety and number of objects; uses one-to-one correspondence to count objects (Crowther, 2018c)

It's important to know the stages that children go through and to understand how they think and how they express their thinking. You can then plan the types of materials to use, how to set up learning activities, and how to provide appropriate language terms, such as "in the middle," "in front of," and *behind*.

Documenting One-to-One Correspondence

Documenting learning is one of the essential elements when planning learning environments and activities. Documentation is important because it provides valuable information to help adults provide the appropriate materials to enhance learning, provide learning spaces to encourage active participation in personal learning, encourage practice of emergent skills, and know what the next steps in the child's learning should be.

Any number of tools could be developed to observe the skill of one-to-one correspondence. The keys to any tool development are the time and effort needed for observing and documenting, the reliability of the tool (does the tool give the same information each time it is used?), and the validity (does the tool actually measure the skill or concept to be measured?). Observations should be made over time in different settings. Ideally, three observations are needed to confirm that the child has successfully consolidated the skill. We'll take a look at a few ways to observe and document one-to-one correspondence:

- Skill chart
- Photographs
- Rubric

Skill Chart

This type of documentation consists simply of the teacher taking notes while observing a child. The notations include the dates and actions performed by the child that indicate that he has mastered a skill.

Sample One-to-One Correspondence Skill Chart

NAME	DATE	SKILL OBSERVED
Danny	09/14/20	Placed pegs side by side on foam rectangle
	09/15/20	Matched 10 vehicles to 10 vehicles on template
	11/12/20	Lined up 15 dinosaurs on blank template, then placed equal number of dinosaurs under set created
Comments: Danny indicated that he had the same number of dinosaurs, but he counted some twice and skipped over some.		

Photographic Evidence

Photos are a useful way to document when a child performs a skill. For each photo, record the date it was taken and describe the child's actions that demonstrate a particular skill. This type of documentation is useful as part of the math section of a child's portfolio.

11/13/20, One-to-one correspondence:

Placed 1 to 5 items on templates

Rubric Development

The advantage of a rubric is that it lists the developmental sequence for a particular skill. All that's needed is to add the relevant comments, photographs, or samples of work. The data gathered will indicate at a glance what level a child has achieved (Crowther, 2018c). Add the photograph, work sample, and/or comment to the appropriate column, along with the date.

Sample Documentation of One-to-One Correspondence

Name: Alexander

LEVELS	COMMENTS
Level 1: Places objects one by one on a linear template using items of the same size, color, and shape	
Level 2: Places objects one by one on a linear template using objects that have more than one difference in size, color, or shape	01/08/20 Counted objects using one-to-one correspondence
Level 3: Places objects one by one on a template in a random order using objects that have more than one difference in size, color, or shape	01/10/20 Counted objects using one-to-one correspondence 01/12/20 Counted objects using one-to-one correspondence 01/15/20 Placed dinosaurs on each of 2 dinosaur mats
Level 4: Places objects one by one on templates of choice (2-D or 3-D) using any objects of choice	

(Crowther, 2018c)

The Facilitator's Role

Adults should observe the everyday activities and actions of the children in order to:

- provide appropriate language concepts, such as indicating that the buses are *under* the planes or the planes are *over* the buses.
- organize materials and resources to encourage one-to-one activities, such as providing linear mats with pictures to encourage children to place one object on each picture.
- use spontaneous activities as teachable moments, such as indicating as you are dressing that you put one arm in one sleeve or one foot in one shoe.
- model counting activities, such as counting objects by placing one finger on an object at a time or moving objects over as they are counted.
- be alert to children who count without using appropriate one-to-one correspondence statetegies, such as missing or skipping over some objects or counting an object twice. When you observe this, model how to count by pointing to each object or moving each object over as you count with the child.

Building One-to-One Correspondence Activities into Routines

Routine activities are a wonderful way to reinforce one-to-one correspondence by observing, redirecting, and providing the language relevant to the activity.

Snack Times and Mealtimes

Set out the appropriate number of materials of plates, cutlery, glasses, serving spoons, placemats, and napkins. Then, encourage the children to set the table. The activity could be done by one child per table or by individual children to set their own places. As the children work, provide language and encourage the children to talk about what they are doing. Reinforce new terms and phrases such as *right*, *left*, *beside*, "at the top," *between*, and "in the middle of." When they're ready, invite children to pour drinks. Describe what they are doing. For example, observe, "Teneshia is holding a jug with her right hand," "Ali is pouring milk into one glass," or

"David is pouring milk from one jug." As they drink, you can say, "Ali is holding one glass in his left hand." "James is drinking from one glass." They can serve themselves with one big spoon and serve food onto one plate. When they help clean up, you can observe, "Sheree is scraping one plate." "Nash is putting one plate into the bin for washing."

Arrival and Departure

Arrivals and departures are ideal times to engage in one-to-one activities with children. It's a particularly excellent time to model and explain the importance of appropriate one-to-one activities to family members.

- **Dressing and undressing:** Identify terms such as *one* and *other* and *first* and *last*: "Edwin, you put on one shoe, then the other shoe." "Aisha put on her jacket *first* and her mittens *last*." Encourage children to identify and describe what they are doing: "I put my pants on first and my boots last. My boots won't fit if I do them first," says Jacob.
- **Putting things away:** Talk about where items belong: on one hook, under one shelf, on one shelf, on top of the shelf, and on the middle shelf.

Transitions

When children are engaged in doing and talking about things, transitions become much smoother and fewer challenging behaviors occur. Encourage children to talk about what they're doing and why their actions are important.

- **Lining up:** Introduce and encourage the children to use vocabulary such as *first*, *middle*, *last*, *beside*, "in between": "I'm in between Carli and Idris. Keith is last. Marisol is first. Then we can go outside," Kim says.
- **Cleaning up:** As they place objects where they belong, describe where the objects are placed—in containers, on shelves, in a corner, in the garbage: "The small block container and the pictures have to be in the center so we can all reach them," explains Jamie.
- **Children talking to each other:** Marisol tells Stephen, "You put the container with the chickens in it on this spot, right on the picture. Then you know where to find it."
- **Helping to set up for the next activity:** As they retrieve items and place them on tables, encourage the children to describe where the items are being placed, such as "in the middle," between two items, and one in front of each chair: Carolina declares, "All done. I put one plate at each spot and one fork beside each plate. That's where everybody sits."

Outdoor Free Play

Outdoor free play is another excellent opportunity to reinforce one-to-one concepts with the children. As they engage in activities, provide the appropriate language and encourage them to talk about what they're doing.

- **Climbing:** As children use climbing rings, climb a ladder, or clamber up a climbing wall, comment on what they are doing: using one hand at a time; using their right hand, then their left hand; holding one rung at a time; alternating hands (called *brachiating*); using one foot at a time; comparing which hand or foot was used first; and so on.
- **Balancing:** When you observe children as they experiment with hopping on one foot, balancing on a beam, or similar activities, describe what you see: hop on one foot and then hop on the other foot, balance on your right foot and then the left foot, use one foot at a time, and so on.
- **Riding:** Describe how children are moving the riding toy: push with one foot at a time, keep one foot on the floorboard and push with the other foot, put one hand on one handlebar and another hand on the other handlebar.
- **Ball skills:** Observe children dribbling or kicking, and comment on what you see: dribbling with your right hand, bouncing the ball with your left hand, kicking with your left foot, dribbling the ball from one hand (or foot) to the other.

Take a look at what materials or equipment is in the children's outdoor space to identify what might be added to encourage more one-to-one correspondence activities.

Building One-to-One Correspondence Activities into Learning Centers

Activities to encourage children's understanding of the one-to-one concept are easy to integrate into your existing learning centers. Keep interest high by adding to or changing the materials from time to time. As the children explore the materials, use terms such as the following when you observe them.

beside	at the beginning	above
behind	on	under
over	part	parallel to
below	in between	first
to the left	at the end	last
in	on top of	adjacent
together	apart	to the right
in the middle	in front	next to

Take photos of the products the children have created and post them for the children to refer to and discuss. Engage them in reflective thinking by asking them to talk about what they have done, what they have learned, what they still need to learn, or what they like or dislike about an activity.

Puzzles and Games Area

Butterfly Matching

Materials

Images of butterflies (2 of each)

Paper

Scissors

Laminator or clear contact paper

Plastic container

What to Do

Print out pairs of images of butterflies and cut them out.

Laminate one of each pair, or cover it with clear contact paper. Trim the excess. Put these in a plastic container.

Cut long strips of paper (3" x 14"). Glue the second of each butterfly pair to the strip. Laminate or cover with contact paper for durability.

Place the materials in the center, and invite the children to explore them and match the butterflies.

Over time, add a variety of different templates and materials, such as shapes, vehicles, flowers, animals, and insects.

Learning in Action

Ms. Kaya observed the children as they engaged in the activity she had set up. She asked Yuvraj what he had done. Yuvraj pointed to items as he explained, "I found a matching butterfly and put one on every single butterfly. It was a bit complicated because you had to look at each butterfly carefully to see that it was the right one. Now every single butterfly has a matching butterfly on it."

As other children gathered around and listened, they decided to try some of the activities themselves. At the end of free play, all the materials were placed on an open shelf, along with a few new ones to encourage continued participation. Children could now choose which materials they wanted to use and bring these to a table.

Kaya: Danny, how did you do your activity?

Danny: Well, I looked at what was on the shelf, but I didn't see stuff I like. So, I took some rocks and pine cones from the science center. Then I put the rocks down in a row. Then I put pine cones on the rocks.

Kaya: What did you learn?

Danny: You had to pick flatter rocks or the pine cones felled off.

Kaya: Anything else you learned?

Danny (scratching his head): Well, I know! If you look at the rocks and pine cones, they're the same number. See each rock has a pine cone, so they're the same.

Block Play

Build a Farm

Materials

Children's book about a farm	Cylinders
Large blocks	Triangular prisms
Small blocks	Rectangular prisms
Unit blocks	Toy animals
Foam blocks	Natural items, such as leaves, twigs, rocks, and so on
Cubes	

What to Do

With the children, read a book about a farm, such as *On the Farm* by David Elliott. Your book choice should focus on the concept of one-to-one correspondence.

Encourage the children to use the materials in the block area to build a farm or homes for the toy animals.

Over time, renew interest by reading new books and adding related items, such as people, vehicles, and traffic signs. Encourage the children to find and use items from anywhere in the classroom environment.

Learning in Action

Marlena decided to create a representation of some of the things she saw in the book about farm animals. She gathered materials she needed from around the room. As she worked, she said to herself, "One duck in the water and one hen in the farmyard and one cow in the muddy field."

KAYA: I see one pig fits under your arch.

MARLENA: They're not arches. It's a gate to the farmyard.

KAYA: Oh, I see. How did you create the gate?

MARLENA: I used three bridge pieces, one in front, one in the middle, and one at the end to make it widest.

KAYA: What other things could fit under the gate?

Marlena picks up a horse, a cow, and a dog and tries each.

MARLENA: Only one animal fits under the gate at a time.

Books to Read to Children

Carle, Eric. 1987. *Have You Seen My Cat?* New York: Simon and Schuster.

Carter, David A. 1990. *Animals.* New York: Simon and Schuster.

Crowther, Ingrid. 2010. *1,2,3 Count.* Edmonton AB: ICC Lifelong Learn Inc.

Martin, Bill, and Eric Carle. 2003. *Panda Bear, Panda Bear, What Do You See?* New York: Henry Holt and Company.

Priddy Books. 2011. *On the Farm.* New York: Macmillan.

Art Center

Art explorations offer excellent opportunities to gain more experience with placement of objects, materials, and creations. Beginning around the age of three, children start to explore where to place objects created on a page. These placements in drawing and painting align very well with one-to-one correspondence. As children work, you can introduce language such as:

- All over the page
- In the middle
- At the bottom
- At the top
- Diagonally across
- On the right-hand side
- On the left-hand side

When children engage in placement activities, adults often tend to encourage them to fill the empty parts of the page. This takes away from children's explorations of placement. Instead, talk to them to let them explain—or describe to them—which placement they have created.

Painting, Drawing, and Printmaking

Materials

Paper in a variety of colors, sizes, and textures

Paint

Paintbrushes

Markers

Colored pencils

Crayons

Chalk

Oil pastels

Stamps

Stamp pads

Easels

Masking tape

What to Do

Provide a variety of surfaces to work on, such as a table, the floor, and on easels and large pieces of butcher paper taped to a wall. This offers children opportunities to see what has been created from different perspectives.

Encourage the children to explore the materials. They may wish to work individually or with one or two friends.

As they explore, comment on what you observe using rich language. Encourage the children to talk about what they are doing.

Take photos of what the children have created and display these aesthetically in the art center.

Learning in Action

KATHY: I made my family. Everyone has one head and one body. Everyone has two arms, but they are on opposite sides.

SOPHIE: I painted one head at the top 'cause that's where heads are. Now I am painting one body under the head.

Sculpting and Collage

Materials

Paper in a variety of colors, sizes, and textures

Playdough

Chenille stems

Boxes

Natural materials

Scissors

Glue

Tape

What to Do

Provide a variety of surfaces on which to work, such as on a table, on the floor, or outside.

Encourage the children to explore the materials. They may wish to work individually or with one or two friends.

As they explore, comment on what you observe using rich language. Encourage the children to talk about what they are doing.

Take photos of what the children have created and display these aesthetically in the classroom.

Learning in Action

Rachel: I am adding a purple rectangle on one side.

Charlie: This is going to be a flag. The green line is first and there's one orange line that is last. Now I am making a long orange line right at the top.

Dramatic Play

Dramatic play is probably one of the most versatile activities to encourage growth and understanding of one-to-one correspondence. Dramatic play affords a variety of planning activities. Work with the children to decide which activity to plan for. List the materials that are available and the materials that are still needed. Decide where in the room to set up and organize the activity. One of the play ideas that is always popular with children is baby care: cooking, feeding, bathing, dressing, going for a walk. It is easy to extrapolate the one-to-one concept from this play and apply it to other play themes in the dramatic play area.

Baby Care

Materials

Baby dolls	Changing table	Baby clothes
Bathtub	Pad	Dresser
Towel	Diapers	Bottles
Soap	Garbage can with lid	Rocking chair
Washcloth	Corn starch	Blankets
Water toys	Cribs	CDs of lullabies
Shampoo	Stroller	Baby books

What to Do

Add the materials to the dramatic play center.

As the children play, observe them and comment on what you see: "Jermaine, I see that you and Miguel are each rocking a baby. You have one baby, and Miguel has one baby."

Comment on children's play to reinforce and model one-to-one activities. For example, encourage naming body parts, such as right foot and arm and left foot and arm. Talk about dressing: one sleeve or pants leg at a time, fit one foot into the foot of the sleeper, slide one button in one buttonhole.

Consider posting a sequence of activity in both pictures and words, such as dressing, undressing, bathing, or feeding, so that the children can refer to the order involved and describe each event using words such as *first*, *next*, and *last*.

Learning in Action

CYDNE: I'm putting on one diaper on her bum.

NADIA: I just gave him a bath. Now I put him in the middle of a towel so I can wrap him up.

Ryan has one baby in his *amauti*, an outfit used by Inuit women to carry a baby in a pouch on the back.

ANNA (to Ryan): I put one sock on each of my baby's feet. Now I am putting the other leg in his sleeper.

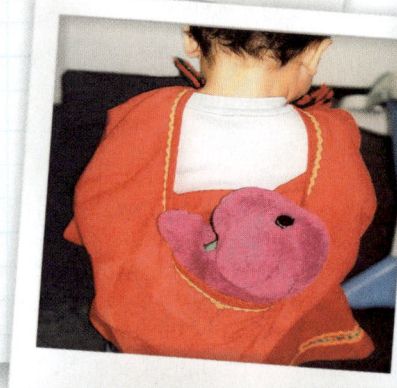

Kitchen

Materials

Table	Spoons	Cutlery
Chairs	Forks	Glasses
Play stove	Spatulas	Highchair
Play oven	Pots and pans	Bibs
Play sink	Measuring cup	Ingredients to cook for baby: flour, water, playdough
Play refrigerator	Recipes in pictures and words	
Bowls	Dishes	
Plates		

What to Do

Add the materials to the dramatic play center.

As the children play, observe them and comment on what you see: "Sarah, I see you're preparing to feed your baby. I see one spoon and one plate."

Consider posting a sequence of activity in both pictures and words, such as feeding, or a recipe, so that the children can refer to the order involved and describe each event using words such as *first*, *next*, and *last*.

Learning in Action

> **JOSH (feeding his baby):** One full spoon.
>
> **MALIK (giving his baby a bottle):** See, that's how you hold a baby's head up. His neck's not too strong.

Manipulatives Area

Manipulative play often involves construction and attachment activities, such as creating a vehicle using magnetic building blocks or attaching Lego pieces together. This area is well suited to establishing understanding of one-to-one correspondence. The manipulatives listed below can support development of these skills.

- Puzzles:
    - » one-piece
    - » interlocking
    - » stacking
    - » cubes
- Construction toys:
    - » magnetic blocks
    - » Legos
    - » Duplos
    - » tree blocks

- » train sets
- » waffle blocks
- » log cabin builders
- » connecting shapes
- » vehicle construction sets
- » small unit blocks
- Miscellaneous materials:
  - » tangram sets
  - » pegboards
  - » dominos
  - » beads
  - » stacking toys
  - » clips
  - » unit cubes
  - » seriation materials
  - » natural materials, such as shells, stones, and pine cones
  - » light table geometric shapes

Organize the area so that the children can easily find what they want to work with and can return the materials to their proper places when they're finished. Provide a table near the manipulatives shelf to give the children an area to work on. A child's ability to complete puzzles depends on the experiences she has had with puzzles. Consider each child's abilities, and choose the materials needed to support the child in further developing her skills.

Provide a variety of puzzles ranging from easy to hard. (See Table 3.2: Puzzles by Age and Stage.) An easy way to accommodate children's ability to choose the correct skill level is to color code the puzzles. Glue a piece of colored paper to the back of each puzzle to indicate which skill level it represents. Provide trays that are color coded in the same way as the puzzles. That way, if a child does not complete a puzzle, she can put the puzzle frame and pieces on the tray so that she can continue to work later. Additionally, storing puzzle frames and their pieces on trays can help prevent the loss of puzzle pieces. Color code the shelf storage system with the same colors as the puzzles, and explain the system to the children. Organize other manipulative materials in a similar way, to maximize appropriate choice and skill levels.

Table 3.2: Puzzles by Age and Stage

AGES AND STAGES	DESCRIPTION
Level 1: One to two years old; color-code back of puzzle and pieces red	• Single large, thick pieces with matching photo on the puzzle board • Easy to grasp and place
Level 2: Two to three years old; color-code back of puzzle and pieces blue	• Single large pieces with knobs and matching photo on the board • Slightly more difficult for little fingers to manipulate into place
Level 3: Three to four years old; color-code back of puzzle and pieces yellow	• Interlocking puzzles with up to 15 pieces • Initially easier if puzzle has a board with a matching background • Increased difficulty when no background exists • Block puzzles: drop shape into predesigned space
Level 4: Four years old and older; color-code back of puzzle and pieces green	• With experience, children can complete interlocking puzzles of increasing size • Stacking puzzles of increasing number of pieces

(Adapted from Crowther, 2018c)

As you observe the children exploring the materials, use terminology to describe what they are doing, such as matching items in sets and comparing sets to identify one more or one fewer. You can describe as they put puzzles together or build, using terms such as *on top of*, *below*, *beside*, *between*, *in the middle*, *at first*, and *at the end*. They can match items by color, size, or shape—for example, "The red part of the connecting puzzle piece fits into the red on the connecting space." As they put construction sets together, you can comment on specific placement of parts—for example, "One wheel at the front, and one on the side," or "One door on each side."

Sidney was very excited that the tops of the markers could fit on her fingers. Ms. LaToya immediately came over and used this as a spontaneous learning situation. She pointed to and identified each colored cap on Sidney's fingers.

Sidney (beaming): One on this finger and this one and this one.

Kendal has been placing one peg in each hole of a pegboard. Then he discovers that he can put the pegs together vertically. His teacher, Leanne, notices Kendal's excitement. She reinforces his understanding by describing the colors he's using.

Leanne: You put one blue one on a red one. Then you put one blue one on top of another blue one. One red peg is in the middle. One purple peg is last.

Liesl has lined up some of her favorite animals. She asks Ms. Yan to come see what she has been doing. As Liesl describes her activity, Ms. Yan writes down what she says.

Liesl: See the panda is between the horses. He is in the middle. The colt is last and the mare is first. The stallion is between the colt and the panda.

Ms. Yan: Is it okay if I take a picture?

Liesl agrees, and Ms. Yan posts the photo in the manipulatives area. This allows Liesl and other children to look at it over time and reflect on the activity.

Dafue has used the tangrams to create the same little girl that another child had created. Ms. Watkins, her teacher, asks her some questions.

Ms. Watkins: I see that you copied Melanie's little girl. Can you tell me about her?

Dafue: She is the same and she's beside Melanie's, but she's facing a different way.

Ms. Watkins: Tell me how you created her.

Dafue: Started by making the head. It is one large square. Then I put one braid on each side of her head. She had one orange shirt. It's a square and one red skirt. It's actually a pentagon. She has two arms and two legs. These are diamonds.

Ms. Watkins: Where are the arms and legs?

Dafue: One arm and one leg on one side and one of each on the other side.

Children expressed interest in dinosaurs. To the manipulative shelf, their teacher, Elena, added matching strips featuring photographs of dinosaurs along with matching dinosaur toys in labeled containers. She encourages Alexander to talk about what he did with the materials.

Alexander (pointing): This one is in the middle of these two. This one is first and this one is last.

During the COVID-19 pandemic, schools were closed, so children were at home, usually learning via distance education. Phoenix had noticed that his brother, Malachi, had been working with a hundred square. He decided that they could produce their own squares by folding a paper. Then they had fun placing objects in each square. The brothers became very inventive in producing one-to-one correspondence using the squared paper they created and objects found around the house. Their mother asked them to talk about how they did their activity.

Phoenix: First you have to fold your paper into squares. Then you simply find objects to place in each square until all the squares have objects in them.

Malachi: I did mine a different way. First, I made a stamp in each square in two rows. Now, I'm putting one cube in each square in the other rows. This time I used only cubes. See? I put a cube in every single square. Each square has a cube in it.

Chapter 3: One-to-One Correspondence

Carpentry

Carpentry experiences offer a wide variety of ways to support and enhance understanding of one-to-one correspondence. Carpentry is also an excellent way to build measurement skills, eye-hand coordination, awareness and understanding of angles, and an understanding of how to handle tools safely. Before children can use real tools and equipment, they need to develop the eye-hand coordination to:

- hammer an object on a specific spot;
- attach things together or pull them apart;
- experiment with wood pieces to sand them or attach items to the wood;
- clamp pieces together before hammering or sawing; and
- wear protective gear.

To afford children a quality experience with carpentry, the following safety practices must apply:

- Set up the area out of the way of classroom traffic.
- Closely supervise when children are engaged in carpentry experiences.
- Provide appropriate eye protection.
- Provide storage to keep tools and materials in a labeled, accessible space.
- Teach the children to put the tools and materials away after use.
- Post simple rules for participation in the area, such as "Put your toys away," with a photo of a child putting a toy away.

Precarpentry Skills

At first, provide materials that will allow the children to explore safely.

Materials

Sturdy wooden workbench

Shatterproof safety glasses

Child-sized gloves (adult sizes are dangerous because proper grip is not possible)

Golf tees

Firm foam

Wooden hammers

Clamps

What to Do

Make sure they use the safety goggles and wear gloves. Encourage the children to explore the materials. For example, let them practice hammering golf tees into the foam, and encourage them to create various patterns or designs. Let them hammer two or more items together and learn to use clamps to stabilize items on the workbench.

As they explore, monitor the area to keep the workbench and the carpentry area free of clutter. Supervise to ensure the children's safety, and reinforce such safe practices as wearing safety equipment. Reinforce handling the materials carefully, such as by placing a golf tee they are using in one spot and hitting it on the head. Help them learn how to appropriately clamp an item to the workbench.

Use rich vocabulary to describe their work, such as "beside each other," "in the middle," and "in the corner." Describe how items are attached to each other: "in the middle," "at the end," "one side overlapping," "one long side," "one short side," "one rectangular piece at the bottom," and "one rectangular piece at the top."

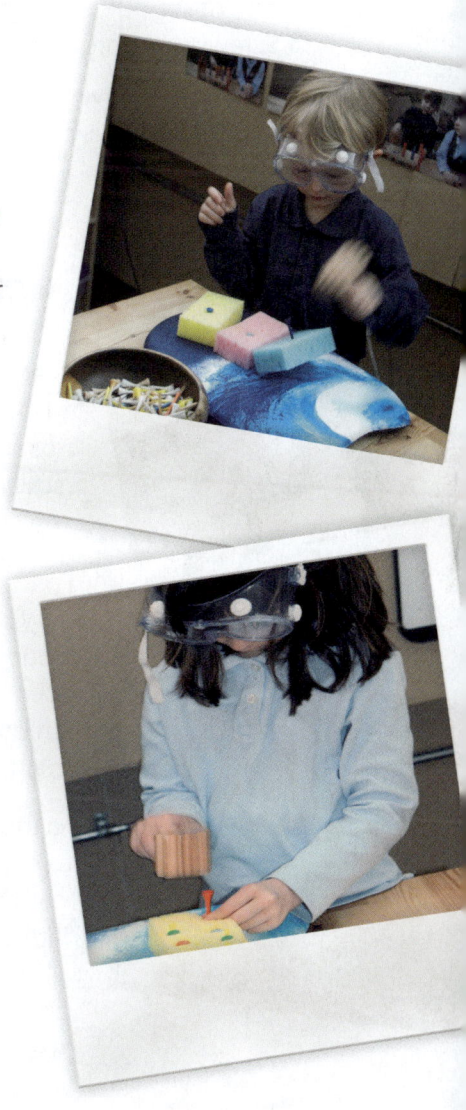

Carpentry Materials and Activities

Once children are able to use the carpentry tools safely and effectively, they are ready to use real carpentry materials.

Materials

Wood—soft wood such as pine

Nails—sturdy, should not bend when hammered; length of nails should be appropriate for width of wood

Screws with large heads

Small screwdrivers—match the heads of screws and fit easily in little hands

Sandpaper in a variety of grits

Miter boxes

Paint

Paintbrushes

Markers

Decorative materials, such as leather, cardboard, and wood chips

What to Do

Initially, prepare pieces of pine ahead of time. For example, get nails or screws started into a 2" x 4" board. This will help the children practice with a hammer or screwdriver and real wood. To make it easier to start sawing, you can also cut grooves in pieces of wood. Help the children clamp the wood to the workbench to keep it stationary.

Show them how to use the miter box so that they can practice cutting on angles. Encourage them to sand the pieces they cut to create smooth surfaces, then use the wood pieces to create 3-D structures.

As they explore, use vocabulary to encourage one-to-one correspondence: "one screwdriver fits into one screw," "one nail fits into one hole," "one hand on the hammer, "one sharp point at one end," and "one groove to cut in."

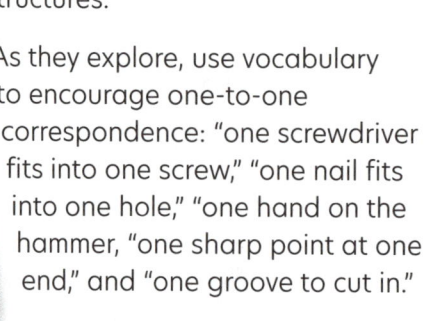

The Path to Early Math

Learning in Action

Miss Jamie: Tell me about your creation.

Haley: It has one ear on one side and one ear on the other side. I screwed it in with one screw at the bottom of each ear, so they can flop. The nose is a piece of satin. I screwed it in the middle with another screw. The rest is just imaginary.

Science

Science and math are closely related; many of the concepts used in math also apply to science. In particular, many skills and knowledge about science concepts also have a base in one-to-one correspondence. Science provides children with many opportunities to make comparisons, which involve comparing one object or situation to another one. When planning for one-to-one correspondence experiences in science, focus on providing opportunities that allow for experimentation, such as working with color and absorption, temperature, length, height, speed, volume, weight, or number. Children must learn to work with one item at a time—which item sinks or floats, dissolves, balances, is longer, is attracted, is heavier, and so on. They must match one item at a time to see if it is the same or different.

Chapter 3: One-to-One Correspondence

Sink or Float

Materials

Water table or large plastic tub

Water

Chart paper

Markers

Real or plastic fruit

Wood pieces

Plastic and metal cutlery

Balls of different densities

Foam blocks

Plastic blocks

Playdough in different sizes and shapes

Shells of different shapes and weights

Objects found on field trips such as stones, pine cones, feathers, or leaves

What to Do

Teach the children that some materials should not be used in water, such as books or wooden building blocks. Otherwise, almost any material will work.

To accurately determine whether an item sinks or floats, the children should test only one item at a time.

Invite them to test a variety of items. Encourage them to create a chart (with your help) to record which items sink and which float.

Learning in Action

Karley, Mapalo, and Keisha decided to see if two oranges, a real one and a plastic one, would float or sink. They tried one orange at a time and were very surprised that the real orange sank and the plastic orange floated.

Suspensions

Materials

Sand
Flour
Ground-up chalk
Mud
Vegetable or mineral oil
Water

Bowls
Clear plastic containers with lids
Clear plastic bottles with lids
Measuring cups
Measuring spoons
Whisks

What to Do

Science activities provide opportunities for learning about different mixtures such as suspensions and solutions. When children create mixtures, encourage them to add one measure of a substance at a time, then stir it with one tool or shake it with one hand.

Suspension materials will float throughout the water when stirred but will eventually settle at the bottom or float at the top.

Suspension or Solution?

In a suspension, the particles mixed into the water will float and then sink to the bottom or float to the top. In a solution, the particles mixed into the water will dissolve.

Solutions

Materials

Water
Salt or sugar
Drink crystals
Food coloring
Liquid or powdered soap
Bowls
Clear plastic containers with lids
Clear plastic bottles with lids
Measuring cups
Measuring spoons
Whisks

What to Do

Invite the children to add salt, sugar, drink crystals, and/or soap to water. Talk with them about what they observe as they explore the materials.

These materials will dissolve in water, leaving it clear or colored. When adding liquid soap, children will notice that bubbles form, but eventually the bubbles will disappear and the water will become clear.

If children add too much of a solid substance, they will notice that some is dissolved and some sinks to the bottom.

Color Mixing

Materials

Tempera paint
Fingerpaint
Watercolor paint
Water
Paintbrushes
Paper or other paintable surfaces or materials
Containers

What to Do

Invite the children to explore making different colors by combining paint colors. Talk with them about what they are doing and what they observe.

Learning in Action

Miss Alvarez covered a table with a plastic tablecloth, then she placed a clear Plexiglas divider on the table.

Miss Alvarez: Alright, everyone. Pick the colors that you want to fingerpaint with.

Jolie decided to use yellow and red paint. She started out by making distinct color shapes on the divider. She discovered that she could mix the colors to get a new color.

Jolie: Look! I just made orange. I mixed red and yellow and got orange!

Color Absorption

Materials

Paper towels

Liquid food coloring in a variety of colors

What to Do

Provide paper towels and food coloring for the children to explore.

Encourage the children to talk about the changes they observe. Display children's efforts along with documentation of what the child observed.

Learning in Action

Anna explained to Michael, "See, you have to take the top off carefully, so you just don't spill it. Then you put a drop on the paper. It's like magic. It explodes into a big drop. See? You can mix colors like I did here."

Balance

Materials

Wooden blocks

Blocks of other materials in a variety of sizes

What to Do

As they explore and build with blocks in the block area, children can learn about creating balanced structures. Any blocks of different sizes and shapes will work. They will find through trial and error that to build a stable structure they need to start with a solid base.

Learning in Action

While Amelia was building her structure, Jan, her teacher, commented on her work.

JAN: I notice how carefully you are placing one block at a time on another one. You are creating a very balanced structure.

When Amelia had finished her structure, Jan asked her about it.

JAN: How did you manage to balance the blocks so well?

AMELIA: See? I put flat blocks on the bottom. If you just use the carpet, the blocks fall. You have to be careful to put the blocks right on top of each other.

Chapter Summary

One-to-one correspondence is the core skill for future success in math development. "Children's initial understanding of quantitative relations is largely based on correspondence. One-to-one correspondence underlies their understanding of cardinality, and one-to-many correspondence gives them their first insights into multiplicative relations" (Nunes, Bryant, and Watson, 2009). When children understand and use one-to-one correspondence, their ability to solve mathematical problems increases. Children who do not understand or gain competence in one-to-one correspondence will struggle with subsequent counting skills and higher math skills.

As they engage in one-to-one activities, they gain not only awareness and skills in one-to-one correspondence but also greater awareness and understanding of spatial relationships. They develop skills in making choices: what to use, how to use it, when to engage in a task, and for how long. They learn to use nontraditional materials to represent their ideas. They develop understanding of science concepts, such as which materials float, and which material can carry items and still float. And they learn to use the strategy of one-to-one correspondence to identify equal or unequal sets.

Apply the Learning

1. Choose and set up an activity area to encourage children to engage in one-to-one activities. What materials will you provide? How could you organize the area?

   Choose a method of documenting the children's learning in the area. Invite the children to explore the area. Observe them, and develop documentation of their learning.

   Post a documentation panel in the area to show evidence of the children's learning.

   Reflect on the success of the documentation panel on children's learning and on family awareness of the learning.

2. Develop a one-to-one-correspondence kit. The kit should include:
   - Well-organized materials
   - Templates and/or containers to encourage independent exploration
   - Observation and documentation techniques to identify children's achievements

CHAPTER 04

Forming Sets

"Building knowledge of equivalence means that children recognise that a group of three apples is numerically equivalent to a group of three oranges, because the number of objects in each group is identical."

—Kate Reid and Nicole Andrews, *Fostering Understanding of Early Numeracy Development*

Sets Defined

A *set* is a collection that contains a specific number of objects. "Before children know how to count, they are able to tell you which of two sets has more without counting" (Shumway, 2011). This ability is related to children's very early creation of sets of objects. As they form sets, they use one-to-one strategies. These sets can range from creating lines of objects to filling templates, such as photos of butterflies, with objects. The process of forming sets supports children's understanding about size, alignment, one-to-one correspondence, and number.

For example, Avion is lining up the large Duplo blocks. He brings the blocks from the block shelf but only picks the large equal-sized blocks. He takes care to line up the blocks perfectly, one at a time, so that the long ends of the blocks fit together.

Elijah is sorting the magnetic animals into like groups. He identifies verbally and by pointing that some sets are equal, such as the rhinos, the kangaroos, and the buffaloes. The set of elephants has the most, and the pandas and giraffes are equal.

Sofi tells her friend Danielle, "All three are the same number. You can tell by just looking, but if you count them, they all have four."

Ages and Stages of Forming Sets

There seems to be a natural order that occurs as children form sets of objects.

Table 4.1: Ages and Stages of Forming Sets

AGE	SKILL DEVELOPMENT
Two to four years old	Forms sets without understanding that this strategy produces sets of equal or unequal numbers; arrangements may be linear or random or filling of templates
Three to four years old	Forms sets to identify which set has an equal number, more, or fewer; comparisons are in linear arrangements as this is a more visual comparison
Four years old and older	Uses a variety of materials to create sets of numbers that are equal or have one more or one fewer in a variety of ways; usually counts the objects to make the sets

(Crowther, 2018c)

Documenting Forming Sets

Documentation strategies include a number of techniques, such as charts and rubrics.

Charts

Charts are a useful tool as they can combine photographs and/or written descriptions of observations. Make observations over time in different settings. Ideally, three observations are needed to confirm that a child has successfully consolidated a skill.

Sample Forming Sets Skill Chart

Name: William

DATE	SKILL	DOCUMENTATION
01/07/2020	Formed equal sets	Used equal-sized vehicles to create a linear set of 3
01/08/2020		Used Tyrannosaurus rex figurines to create linear equal sets of 5
01/09/2020		Used cubes to create equal horizontal structures of 10 cubes

Comments: William indicated that the sets were equal.

Interpretation: William has gained understanding of equal sets.

Rubrics

As described in chapter 3, a rubric lists the developmental sequence for a particular skill. All that's needed is to add the relevant comments, photographs, or samples of work. The data gathered will indicate at a glance what level a child has achieved (Crowther, 2018c).

As children accomplish specific skills and concepts, record the information in the rubric and share it with them. This gives them a sense of pride in accomplishment. Then, when you meet with parents or family members, share and explain each child's individual, documented progress.

> William was very proud that he had completed level two of the rubric. When his mother came to pick him up, William showed her the progress he'd made. William's mom told her son how impressed she was with his accomplishment. Later, as she reviewed the rubric more closely with William's teacher, she was able to clarify why this was an important skill for William to learn.

Rubrics also help children build an awareness of what they have learned and what is still to be learned: "I know how to makes things equal," William said. "Now I'm gonna make sets with one more."

Sample Rubric for Forming Sets

Name: William

LEVEL 1	LEVEL 2	LEVEL 3	LEVEL 4	LEVEL 5
Forms sets without understanding that this strategy produces sets of equal or unequal numbers; arrangements may be linear or random or filling of templates	Forms sets to identify whether they are equal or unequal in number; compares different linear sets up to 5 9/16/2020: 9/18/20: Repeated creating equal set using 5 people on 2 rectangular blocks	Forms sets to identify which set has an equal number, more, or fewer; compares different linear sets up to 5	Forms sets to identify which set has an equal number, more, or fewer; compares different linear sets up to 8	Forms sets to identify which set has an equal number, more, or fewer; compares different linear sets up to 10

Comments: 09/23/2020: William was very proud of himself. "I know what *equal* means. All the same number."

Summary of Rubric Documentation
William has completed level 2 of forming sets. He is aware of what he knows and also indicated that he will try to do some sets that are "unequal."

Building Understanding of Different Sets

Children gain understanding of building sets by manipulating real objects, using one-to-one correspondence strategies, and having their activities acknowledged and reinforced. If they have interesting materials to support their activities, they're more likely to engage in creating sets of different objects. Provide opportunities for independent choices that incorporate the children's interests.

Almost daily, Yuvraj and Alexander use math materials to create sets of different types. Their teacher, Jasmine, noticed their interest and asked them to describe what they were creating.

Yuvraj: You can see they're all the same. See, they have the same number, colors, and they're all rectangles.

Alexander: I made four different sets. Two are the same. See (pointing to sets of two)? These only have two each, but these have a lot more (pointing to sets of six).

Provide opportunities for children to reflect on their discoveries. Jasmine posted the photos she had taken of the children's explorations of creating sets. Later, she saw that Yuvraj was looking at his photo, so she asked him what he thought about what he had done. He said he wanted to make it again, and off he went to find the same materials.

Jasmine: How will you make it today?

Yuvraj: I'm going to use the same blocks. I am going to make a different design.

Once he had completed his new design, Jasmine asked, "How did you make it differently?"

Yuvraj: It is a different design, and the first one (pointing at the photo) has the same number, but the second one has more.

Jasmine: What have you learned?

Yuvraj: If you make things the same, it is easy to tell if they are the same or if they are not. You don't even have to count!

Chapter 4: Forming Sets

Materials for Forming Sets

Offer materials for a wide range of choices for all developmental abilities. This way, the child has to engage in some initial planning and decide what materials he wants to use and then bring them to the location of choice.

- Counters
- Toy animals, such as sea life, farm animals, pets, insects, wild animals, dinosaurs, and birds
- Toy vehicles, such as cars, trains, buses, and trucks
- Clothes pegs in a variety of colors
- Buttons of different sizes and colors
- People figurines
- Natural materials, such as flowers, leaves, shells, pine cones, gems, and stones
- Geometric shapes in a variety of sizes and colors
- Light table plastic shapes
- Plates, glasses, cups, cutlery, pots, and pans
- Large unit blocks, small colored unit blocks
- Mats in a variety of shapes
- Linear mats

Mats encourage children to place items on them. You can make linear mats from construction paper cut into 3" x 12" strips and laminated or covered with clear contact paper. You can also make mats in a variety of shapes (circles, squares, triangles) and larger mats that are wide enough to hold two sets. Pay attention to the children's interests and, if possible, add materials that reflect those interests.

Organization

Store materials by type, color, and size, so children can readily find the materials they want to use. There is no need to dump out the materials to find the desired items. Organize the materials in clear containers on open shelves, and label them with words and photos by the type of material. Provide a table near the area that is clear of materials to encourage the children to choose what they want to use, and provide a clear, carpeted area where they can align large unit blocks.

The Facilitator's Role

The facilitator's role is critical. Encourage set building by helping the children develop their skills. Observe and document each child's abilities, then use the information you gather to provide the appropriate materials and experiences to meet each child's skill and ability level.

Reinforce the children's learning by using appropriate language to help consolidate their concept development, such as *equal, more than/less than, one more/one fewer*. Use teachable moments when they occur.

> Lana had created two sets. The sets looked quite different, but with careful observation, it was evident that the sets contained an equal number. Her teacher, Jessica, noticed that Lana had created equal sets and asked her about them.
>
> **Jessica:** Tell me about what you've done.
>
> **Lana:** See, I made two sets. They are very different, but they are equal.
>
> **Jessica:** How did you do that?
>
> **Lana:** I made them at the same time. I put one block down on one, then one on the other.
>
> Jessica asked Lana to share what she had done with the rest of the children at her table. The children listened carefully. Jessica noticed that some of the children started to create sets of equal numbers of blocks that were aligned differently, as Lana had done.

Chapter 4: Forming Sets

Encourage children's interest by creating displays that reinforce concept and skill development. For example, if the children are interested in dinosaurs, create displays of materials involving dinosaurs. Plan with the children. They have good ideas about their interests and the materials they'd like to use. Accept their suggestions and ideas, and implement them as much as you are able. If they take the initiative and collect items that could be used in making sets, include the items on the math shelf. For example, during the Christmas season, the children had formed sets as they decorated templates of Christmas trees. Chase brought in some small, colorful pompoms to use. As children explore the materials and create sets, encourage them to reflect on their learning and thinking.

Planning Introductory Activities

Consider the following as you think about how to engage children in investigating ways to form sets. In the beginning, the materials should be of the same relative size. When children are comparing sets and the sizes are different, they can easily get confused and identify a set that looks bigger or longer as having "more." For example, Marlena consistently identified the set of snowflakes as having more, even though she counted the two sets and got the same answer. Marlena is still confused by the appearance of her set. To her, if it looks longer, it *is* longer and therefore has more items.

To avoid this type of confusion, provide same-size materials, and point out to the children to visualize how the materials:

- are similar: "How are the objects the same?" Or, pointing to an object: "See? This object is the same size as the other one."
- fit together: "Let's put the objects side by side to see if they are the same."
- fit into a space: "How many objects could we put into this space?"

According to Hattie, Fisher, and Frey (2017), children need to gain surface skills before they can engage in deeper learning. Observe the children to identify their stages of development, and plan activities that will help them build their understanding. For example, Ms. Yan observed the three- and four-year-old children as they played with different figures in the manipulatives center. She noted a range of skills and abilities in forming sets.

- Level 1, random arrangements of objects
- Level 2, comparing linear sets: When comparing sets, children need to be able to make independent choices so they can demonstrate their understanding of what types of sets they have created: equal, more, or fewer. The ability to count objects provides greater ability to compare the sets created. Adults need to remember that children at the egocentric stage will find it more difficult to compare objects if the objects are of different sizes. For example, both Marlena and Naomi were able to accurately count the sets they had created. But Marlena was still confused about what she saw rather than what she counted.

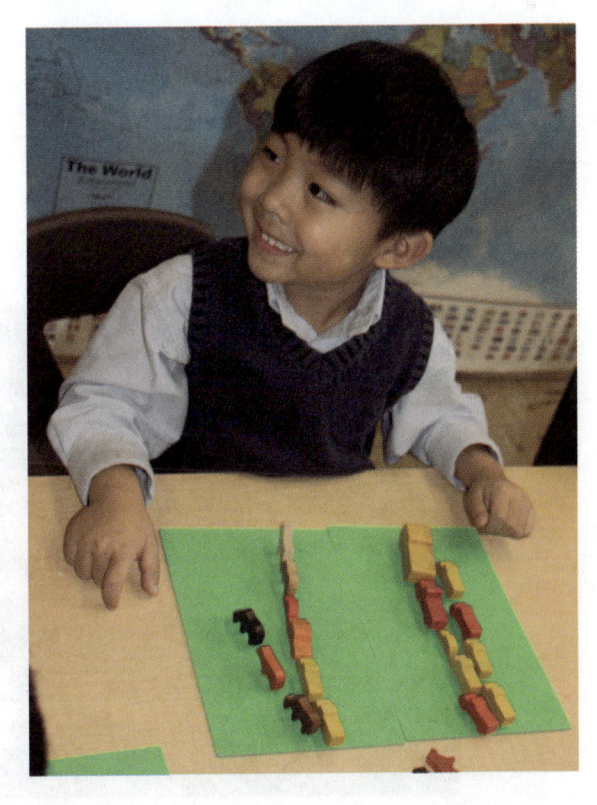

Chapter 4: Forming Sets

Ms. Yan had recently noticed that the children were interested in farm animals and vehicles, so she planned a new activity to capitalize on this interest and nurture their understanding of creating sets. She gathered the following materials:

- Clear plastic bins
- Labels (both photo and word)
- Toy vehicles, such as cars, trucks, buses, planes, and trains
- Toy farm animals, such as geese, ducks, horses, cows, pigs, dogs, cats, and goats
- Linear mats (3" x 12" pieces of paper, laminated)
- Circular mats in a variety of colors
- Rectangular mats in a variety of colors

She placed the toy vehicles and farm animals into separate clear plastic bins and labeled each type of toy with both words and pictures. She put the bin of toy vehicles on one table and the bin of farm animals on the other table. Next, she set out mats in different sizes and shapes on each table.

She pointed out the new materials to the children and speculated, "I wonder what you could do with them." She reminded the children that she would take some photographs of what they were doing. She also asked them to clean up before they left the tables.

The children came to the activities by choice. As they explored, Ms. Yan and her coteacher, Ms. Sasha, engaged with the children, taking photographs and saying, "Tell me about what you created." Marlena created two linear sets. She said that the snowflakes in one made a longer set, so it had more. Even when she counted six in each set, she still insisted that the snowflakes had more. Jayden choose two rectangular mats. He created linear, random sets and said, "They are all lined up."

Kiyaan and Naomi brought some blocks and people to the table. They wanted to see how many people could sit on the block. Naomi declared, "I counted six. What did you get?" Kiyaan replied, "I don't know." Adelyn chose a mat. She said, "I used up all my cars and planes and buses. There's still room for more."

Next, Ms. Yan decided to involve the children in the planning process to set up a math environment that encouraged set building. She posed the following questions to the children and noted their responses.

- "What materials would you like to use to build sets?" In addition to the vehicles and small colored blocks, the children wanted:
    » "I would like to see the little dinosaurs."
    » "Little and the big bears."
    » "I think we could use the shells we collects."
    » "We could go out and collect stones."

Chapter 4: Forming Sets

- » "How about buttons too?"
- » "Make prints with paint."
- » "What about the sea animals?"
- » "The people."
- » "Can we have some shape mats like triangles or circles too?"
- "Where should we keep the materials?"
  - » All the children agreed that they should use the math shelf.
- "Where do you think you'd like to work?"
  - » "I think we can work on the math table."
  - » "I think we could work on the carpet in the block center. That way we can use the blocks there."
  - » "How about wherever we like?"
- "What rules should we set?"
  - » "Ask to have a photograph taken of what we have done."
  - » "Clean up when you are done so that it doesn't look messy."
  - » "Go wherever you want to work."
  - » "If you're not finished, put a sign up to save."

With the information gathered from the children and the observations made, Ms. Yan and Ms. Sasha collected the materials, placed them in labeled containers, and placed the containers on labeled spots on the math shelf.

The teachers took photos of the children's activities and created a book. They glued each photo to a piece of paper and then asked each child to talk about what he or she had created. They wrote the children's responses underneath the photos. They slid each page into a clear sleeve and put the sleeves into a three-ring binder. They placed the book on the math shelf for easy access. Ms. Yan and Ms. Sasha encouraged the children to look at what they had accomplished or what someone else had done and to reflect upon what they wanted to achieve next.

> Naomi was looking in the book at her picture. She had lined up all the farm animals on a linear mat. Ms. Sasha saw her looking at her photo and asked Naomi to reflect on what she had done.
>
> **Ms. Sasha:** What do you like about what you did?
>
> **Naomi:** I like how they are all lined up in a straight line. I like the way the horses and the lambs and the pigs are all together.
>
> **Ms. Sasha:** If you do it again, would you do it the same way?
>
> **Naomi:** I am going to do it again. I am going to do it on a larger mat. I think I want to match all the animals 'zactly.
>
> **Ms. Sasha:** Why do you want to do it this way?
>
> **Naomi:** I want to see if I have enough animals to do it.
>
> Naomi got all the materials she needed and completed her task.
>
> **Ms. Sasha:** Well, tell me what you liked about the new way you did this.
>
> **Naomi:** It worked. See? All the animals match and I had enough animals. There's still some left over.
>
> **Ms. Sasha:** What did you learn?
>
> **Naomi:** You can do things differently and it's still fun. You have to look at what you did before and think about a different way.

Planning for Comparison Sets

When children begin to compare sets (level 2), they are demonstrating that they are ready for more than simply grouping items in random ways. The materials for this activity are the same as those listed on page 86. Store the materials where the children can easily access them; in Ms. Yan's class, this is on an open, accessible shelf as indicated in the children's plans.

Comparing sets is much easier for the children if they compare items in a linear fashion and if the items are of the same relative size. Supply mats that are wide enough to hold two linear sets, or let the children use two linear mats of equal size to compare their sets.

As they explore the materials and engage in comparing the sets they make, reinforce their learning with appropriate language:

- Equal sets
- Unequal sets
- Sets that have more objects
- Sets that have fewer objects
- One more
- One less

Give the children free choice in what activities to engage in. They know what they already know and what they still need to learn; they will choose activities, from the materials provided, that are at their level. Encourage the children to share their discoveries. This not only reinforces the individual child's competence and positive self-image but also provides other children with opportunities to become aware of new concepts and skills. They can share discoveries in many different ways:

- Posting photographs in books or on boards to allow children to review and reflect on them at different times
- Verbally sharing with the group what they have accomplished
- Posting new learnings in a central location to share with family members
- Having their teacher draw their attention to peers' new or innovative learning

The children in Ms. Yan's class chose their activity, found the materials they wanted to work with, and chose their work location independently. Alayna made one linear set of dinosaurs. "They're all the same," she explained. She then got another strip and duplicated her effort. She decided to make her sets "unequal," pointing as she said, "This one has one more."

"This is equal," Haeran said. "You can tell just by looking. I'm going to make it equal again, but this time it will be different. One cube then one circle all the way up. It's all equal."

Brennan and Sebastien worked collaboratively to form equal sets. The boys planned which materials to use, where to work, and how to represent their sets. As they built, they compared each step of the process. Both boys were very excited when they had completed the task.

Brennan: They are equal, but I used different colored blocks.

Sebastien: Yeah, they are equal. You just have to look.

Chapter 4: Forming Sets

When the family members arrived to pick them up, the children would often excitedly lead them to the photos of their activities and elaborate on what they had accomplished. Often, family members do not have a clear idea why children engage in some of these activities. To help them understand the importance and the learning of the posted activities, add interpretations of the concepts that the children are exploring, such as the following:

- Through activities that reinforce one-to-one correspondence, children learn to recognize that an object holds a unique spot in any set.
- As children gain experiences with forming and comparing sets, their ability to form and recognize sets of different types increases. Through this activity, they also gain experiences in using one-to-one correspondence techniques to begin to count objects.
- As children form equal and unequal sets, they gain a greater number sense and understanding of the concepts of *equal* and *unequal*.
- Understanding "one more" and "one fewer" are important skills in learning to count.
- As they fill templates, they gain experiences with spatial orientation that lead to future understanding of measurement, such as *area* and *perimeter*.

As Haeran's understanding developed, she explored creating unequal sets. She explained, "I made two sets of people sitting down on pretend logs. At first, I just wanted to see how many people I could place on a log. Then I decided to make unequal sets. So, I got another log, but I put fewer people on it. You can tell there's less 'cause there is a space on the second log."

As children's understanding grows and deepens, they are able to begin to use templates that provide opportunities to form other types of sets. Provide objects that are organized by category but differ in size, shape, or color. For example, a set of objects in a variety of sizes encourages children to match objects by size, comparing to create equal sets. Alexander and Brennan matched the sizes and shapes of the blocks they used.

As children create their sets, they will visualize the number of objects in each set to identify whether they are equal, have more, or have fewer. For example, Annie excitedly exclaimed, "See? They are all the same! You can tell!"

Children will use one-to-one correspondence to form sets. For example, Annabel carefully placed one animal at a time on each mat, to match the numbers on the two mats.

Provide mats of different sizes and shapes. When children use mats of different shapes, they not only gain knowledge about shapes but also learn how to compare sets in different configurations.

The block area presents a marvelous opportunity to coordinate activities and materials to engage in forming sets of different numbers. In particular, small unit blocks of various colors are excellent materials to form and compare sets.

Challenge Cards: Equal, More Than, Fewer Than

Materials

Camera

Computer with printer

Colored unit blocks in a variety of sizes

Marker

Paper

Construction paper

Clear contact paper or laminator

What to Do

Build several different block structures, and take a photo of each.

Print the photos. Glue each one onto a piece of construction paper.

On one, write *equal*. On another, write "1 more than." On another, write "1 fewer than." Continue until you have used all the photos to create challenge cards.

Cover each challenge card with clear contact paper or laminate for durability.

Place the challenge cards in the block area. Initially, you may have to help the children understand what to do. After that, they will likely want to make their own challenge cards for their classmates.

Learning in Action

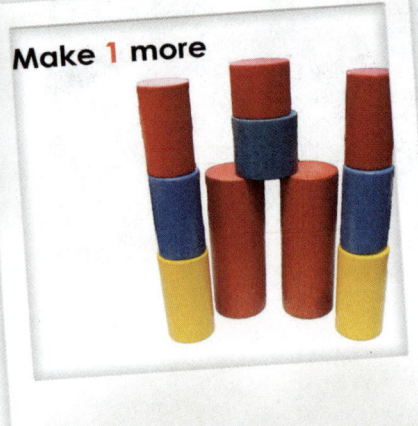

Ms. Yan observed that the children in her class were creating interesting structures with the small, colored unit blocks. She decided to take photographs of the structures they created. She then made challenge cards to encourage the children to create sets that were equal to, more than, or fewer than the set in the photograph.

To help the children understand the instructions and provide visuals of the challenge, Ms. Yan created display cards that she placed in a challenge book in the math area. For example, she placed two block structures that were of equal size on a card along with the word *equal*. She encouraged the children to look at the cards to see what kind of challenge they wanted to engage in. The children enjoyed the challenge activity and quickly asked to have photographs taken so that they could help to create new challenge cards.

Lily Pad Comparisons

Materials

Green foam sheets

Scissors

Plastic frogs, dragonflies, or ladybugs

Tub or water table

Water

What to Do

Cut the foam into lily-pad shapes.

Put the lily pads and frogs or insects next to the water table or tub.

Encourage the children to form equal or unequal sets of frogs or insects on the various lily pads. Children tend to begin with small numbers of objects to use as comparisons, but as their skills and abilities increase, they create larger and larger sets.

Learning in Action

Children explored how big a set could be before the lily pad sank. This led to exploring concepts of one more or one fewer. "Oops, I guess that was one too many. The lily pad is sinking."

Chapter Summary

As children form sets, they gain many valuable skills to learn to object count—counting objects to correctly answer the question of how many objects are within a set. These skills include:

- One-to-one correspondence
- Identifying sets that are equal, unequal, and have more or fewer items
- Gaining experiences in how to create number comparisons that do not rely on actual counting

Apply the Learning

1. Children of a similar age group are not necessarily at the same skill level, nor will they demonstrate their learning in the same way. Think about ways you might organize a math area to accommodate the various skill levels of your age group. Consider the following:
   - The types of materials to provide
   - How to organize the materials
   - How children will access the materials

2. You notice that three children are engaged in forming unequal sets. They ask you to join them, and they are talking about which sets have more or fewer objects. What vocabulary might you provide to extend their learning?

3. Consider ways to encourage children to form sets during outdoor playtime.
   - What materials might you encourage the children to take outside?
   - What questions might you ask to encourage the children to create sets?
   - Where might these activities take place?

4. How could you respond to a parent who asks you to explain why her child is spending so much time making sets? What explanation would you give about the value of this activity? How could you use this opportunity to explore this topic with other families?

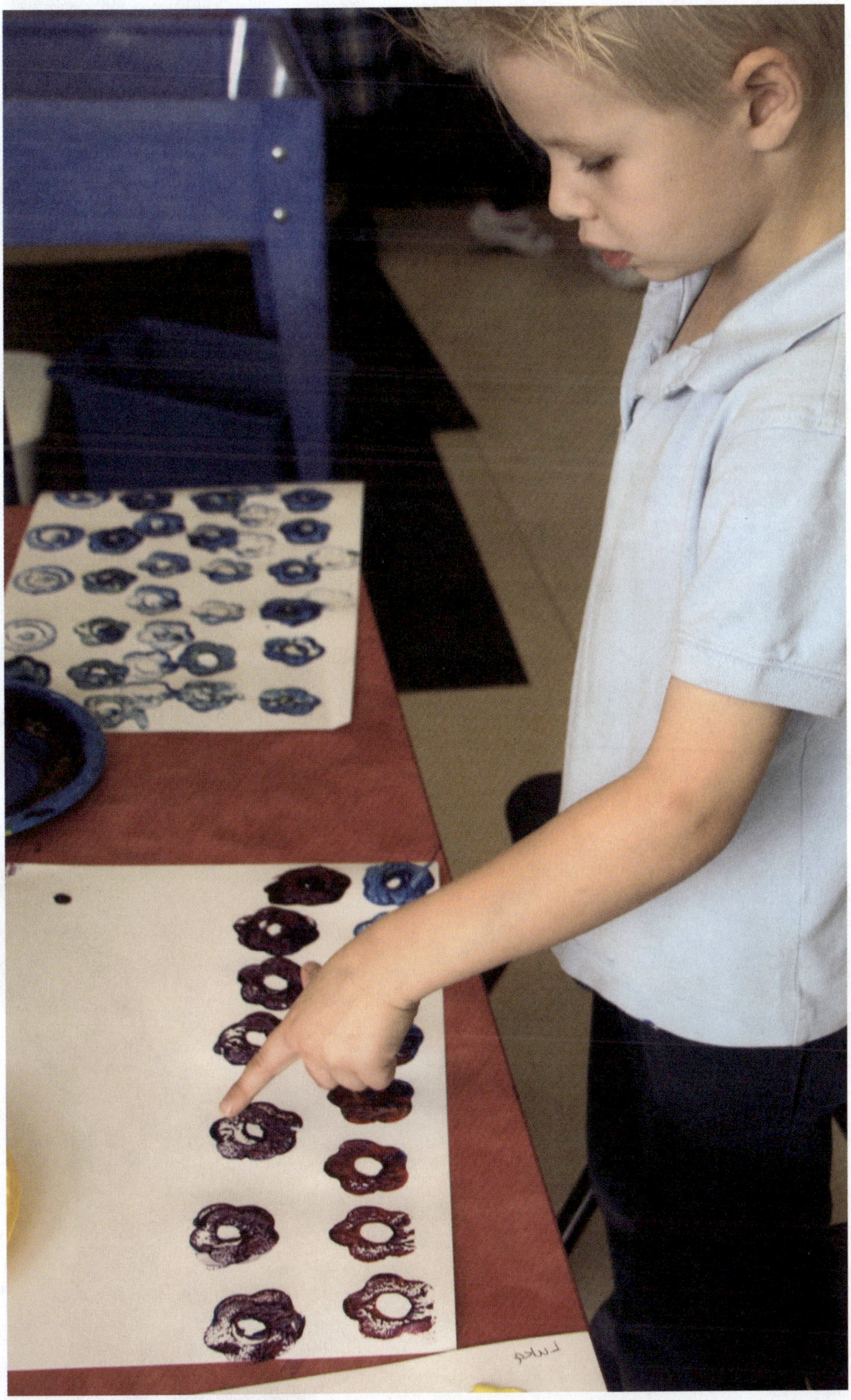

CHAPTER 05

Object Counting

"Count a set of objects with a young child, move objects and count them again, and they will be enchanted by the fact they still have the same number."

—Jo Boaler, *Mathematical Mindsets*

Object Counting Defined

Object counting refers to the ability of a child to count a set of objects and identify accurately how many items have been counted. The ability to count objects accurately depends on the following skills and abilities.

- **One-to-one correspondence:** This is the idea that only one object occupies a defined space and that in a set of objects, only one object is identified by a specific number.
- **Number Sequence:** This refers to the understanding that numbers are arranged in a certain order. At this point, children may not realize that numbers refer to a specific number of objects.
- **Forming sets:** This may include counting objects in sets to identify how many.
- **Understanding terms:** Terms such as *equal*, *more*, and *fewer* are important as children develop counting skills.
- **Counting objects:** The child understands that the last number counted represents the number of items counted.
- **Ordinals:** The child can pick out the position of a number within sets of numbers, such as the middle, first, or last.
- **Number recognition:** Children can identify and print numbers.
- **Understanding that higher numbers represent greater quantities**
- **Conservation:** Children begin to understand that, no matter how objects in a set are arranged, the number of objects stays the same.

Carla, a five-year-old, was able to count accurately to twenty. After she had put some leaves on her tree, she counted them to see how many she had. Finally, she stopped and took all the leaves off the tree. She lined them up in a straight line. When asked why she did this, she replied, "When I count them on the tree, I get different numbers every time I count them. When I put them in a straight line, it's easier to count. See? I can move them over, and I know I counted that leaf.

> Mikel and Amy were discussing numbers.
>
> **AMY:** I know that one hundred is more than ten or even ninety.
>
> **MIKEL:** Yeah, but a zillion is even much more. It is the biggest number.
>
> **ANNA:** I have five planes.
>
> **JORDYN:** They both have three exactly!

Ages and Stages of Learning to Count

Researchers and educators, such as the National Association for the Education of Young Children (2002), the Canadian Child Care Federation (2009), the National Council of Teachers of Mathematics (2000), and Douglas Clements and

Julie Sarama (2009), have identified when and how children typically learn to count. It is important to recognize that the ages and stages represent averages. Depending on a child's experiences with object counting, she may exceed these averages or be delayed in her abilities.

Table 5.1: Ages and Stages of Learning to Count

AGES	SKILLS AND ABILITIES
Two to three years old	• Rote counting: Recites numbers from one to ten but may not be in correct order • Ordinals: Identifies first and last
Three years old	• Rote counting: Recites numbers from one to ten • Counting objects: Skipping or double counting are common errors
Four years old	• Rote counting: Recites numbers from one to ten • Counting objects: Counts accurately to five
Five years old	• Rote counting: Recites numbers to twenty • Counting objects: Counts to ten; counts backward from ten; continues to count from various starting points, such as three or five or six, to ten; represents sets of numbers to ten diagrammatically; identifies next number to twenty or thirty • Ordinals: Uses *first*, *second*, *third*, *fourth*, and *fifth* correctly
Five to six years old	• Counting objects: Identifies the number before and after a given number; skip counts by tens, fives, and twos; counts backward from ten by five years old and from twenty by six years old; starts counting at any number to twenty • Ordinals: Uses *first* to *tenth* correctly • Conservation: Counts objects to thirty in different arrangements

The Facilitator's Role

The primary role of the facilitator is to observe children as they engage in tasks and to step in and support a child's activity when needed. You can do this in a number of ways:

- Support the child's ability to count.
- Provide opportunities to problem solve.
- Use spontaneous teaching opportunities when they arise.

Support the Child's Ability to Count

Alexander was struggling with counting. His teacher, Ms. Reba, acknowledged Alexander's efforts positively and modeled the correct number sequence.

> **Alexander:** One, two, four, five, six buses.
>
> **Ms. Reba:** Let's try this together.
>
> They pointed and counted together.
>
> **Ms. Reba:** You have five buses.
>
> Alexander decided to count again.
>
> **Alexander (holding up his fingers):** One, two, three, four, five. Five buses.

Provide Opportunities to Problem Solve

As Jacob tried to count the animals on a photo card, his teacher Jonathan noticed that he was getting frustrated.

JONATHAN: You seem to have a problem. Can I help you?

JACOB: I keep forgetting what I counted.

JONATHAN: What could you do to solve this problem?

Jacob thought about it and quickly ran to the math center. He brought back a box of numbers.

JACOB: I can put a number under each one.

Jacob tried this strategy and was excited when it worked.

This activity reinforced not only Jacob's ability to solve problems but also his ability to count objects in a random distribution, match number symbols to the objects counted, and identify how many objects he had counted.

Use Spontaneous Teaching Opportunities

Carly picked up a phonics book to look at and noticed that a page showed different animals. She started counting them. Carly had just started to count objects to five. Her teacher Laura noticed her counting and quickly sat down beside her.

> **Laura:** Wow, you counted all the animals. What else could you count?
>
> Carly and Laura continued to count various items on the page.

This activity reinforced Carly's emerging counting skills.

Documenting Learning to Count

Documentation provides valuable information to help adults provide appropriate materials, learning spaces, and encouragement for children. Documentation can also help children reflect on what they have learned and understand what they still need to learn.

There are several ways to document children's emerging counting skills, such as individual number books, a graph, a checklist, and a rubric.

Individual Number Books

An excellent way to document children's learning is to create individual number books for them. Each book should contain a record of the math activities the child has engaged in, such as drawing objects, along with the number symbols of how many objects are drawn, and photographs and explanations of the child's math activities. These books will provide opportunities for the children to reflect on past learning, review the skills and abilities they have accomplished, and identify what they need to learn.

Graphs

Children should be considered protagonists in their own learning, meaning that they should be more aware of why they need to learn something, what they have learned, what they still need to learn and work on, and what they excel at. They're ready to engage in self-learning when they have reached the following skills levels:

- Read number symbols to at least ten
- Engage in object counting to at least three
- Show independence in counting activities

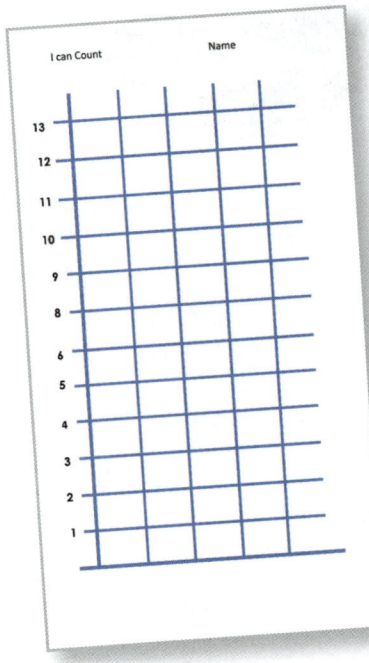

Teach the children how to graph their own learning. To start, create a folder for each child, and store the folders in an accessible place. Create an individual grid for each child, and place one in each folder.

With the children, discuss what a graph is and how it is used. Explain that when a child has created and counted a set of objects, she can go get her graph out of her folder and fill in the appropriate squares. Demonstrate how to fill in a graph. For example, if a child has made a set of five objects and counted them, she would color in five squares or would put an X in five squares (starting at the bottom in the left-hand column and filling in squares up to the number five). Then, the teacher fills in the date and initials the bottom of the column. When the children are ready to proceed on their own, they can tell their teacher when they have made and counted a set, and the facilitator can check their learning.

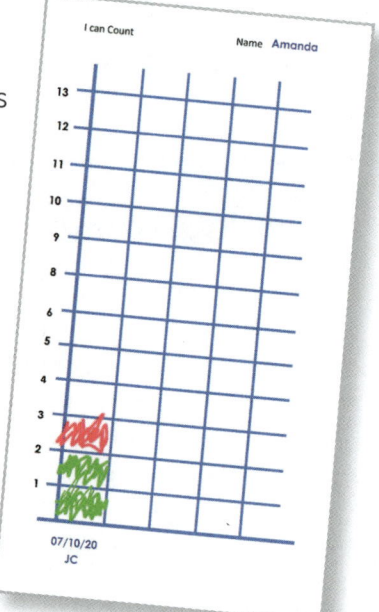

Later, when their families come to the classroom, the children can show their graphs and talk about what they have learned and what they intend to do next. This makes family members aware of their children's progress and provides opportunities to support the learning at home.

Checklists

When you observe a child demonstrating counting, record the date and any relevant comments.

The blank square can be used for recording numbers beyond ten that a child counts to. For a child to qualify as having mastered counting to a certain number, you should observe her counting that number of objects at least three times in three different settings.

Sample Counting Checklist

Name: Amanda

NUMBERS COUNTED TO	DATES/ COMMENTS	NUMBERS COUNTED TO	DATES/ COMMENTS
0		6	
1		7	
2		8	
3		9	
4		10	
5	07/10/20— Initiated activity; 09/10/20; 11/4/20		

Chapter 5: Object Counting

Rubric

The rubric documentation is easy to use and can include artifacts such as photos and notes about comments the child has made explaining her thinking. Attach photos and other information to the rubric for each child. This evidence validates that the child has accomplished the counting skill.

Sample Documentation of Object Counting

Object Count: Ability to count objects and accurately identify how many have been counted

Name: Amanda

Level 1	Level 2	Level 3	Level 4
Counts objects to 3 and indicates "I have 3"	Counts objects to 5 and indicates "I have 5"	Counts objects up to 7 and indicates how many there are	Counts objects up to 10 and indicates how many there are
self graph 1 - 7/10	checklist 1 - 2 2x, 9/10		

Comments:

Building Understanding of Number Sequence

Children between two and three years old begin to recite numbers, but not necessarily in the correct order (Clements and Sarama, 2014). For example, three-year-old Jeremy counts his cars saying, "One, two, three, five, six." Understanding the sequence of the numbers is important in developing the ability to:

- count objects and accurately answer the question of how many have been counted,
- arrange a number of items in ascending or descending order,
- count and compare sets of objects to identify how these sets are similar or different, and
- build foundations for later math skills such as estimating and measuring.

Planning for Number Sequencing

Often young children learn number sequencing by memorization. This leads to rote counting—saying the number names—but does not mean that the child associates the meanings of the numbers with the names. Learning the number sequence is more meaningful when you embed the understanding in activities, such as the daily routine. Think about ways to incorporate modeling and counting with children during activities such as the following:

- When walking up and down stairs, count each step.
- When setting the table, count each item as you place it on the table: One, two, three, four forks.
- During clean-up activities, count the number of blocks a child carries, the number of clothes the children hang up on hooks, or the number of balls they put back in a basket.
- During outside play, count the number of steps up a ladder, the number of pushes on a swing, or the number of times running around an obstacle.
- During mealtimes, count the number of spoonfuls eaten, the number of servings, or the number of green items to eat.

When children are engaging in one-to-one-correspondence or set-building activities, use these as spontaneous opportunities to model and encourage counting in sequence.

> Arianna is playing with toy cars in the block area. Miss Jennifer notices and says, "I wonder how many there are. Let's count them together."
>
> She and Arianna point at each car and count, "One, two, three, four, five."
>
> Arianna declares, "We counted five cars."

If a child skips or double counts items, say, "Let's try this again. Make sure you put a finger on each item as you count." Sing or chant songs, such as "This Old Man," with the children. Read rhymes, such as "One, Two, Buckle My Shoe," or books, such as *Ten Apples Up on Top* by Dr. Seuss. See the resources section on pages 135–145 for other suggestions.

Building Understanding of Ordinals

Ordinal numbers describe the position of something in a list or linear alignment: first, second, third, last, and so on. Young children learn the terms *first*, *second*, and *last* very early (Clements and Sarama, 2009). Teaching young children about ordinal values depends on using these terms in everyday experiences, such as lining up, dressing, cooking, running a race, and retelling stories. For example, as children get ready to go outdoors on a frosty day, comment, "We put snow pants on first and gloves last." When children line up to go out to the playground, say for example, "I see that Maria is first, Devon is second, Mei Ling is third, Teneshia is fourth...," ending with, "and Tony is last." When you read a story to the group, ask the children, "What happened first?" and "What happened next?" Continue in this manner until the children have retold the story.

> As the children followed a recipe for making ants on a log, Mr. David read the steps aloud. "First, we wash our hands. Second, we each put a piece of celery on our plate. Third, we get a spoonful of cream cheese. Fourth, we spread the cream cheese on the celery. Fifth, we get a handful of raisins. Sixth, we put the raisins on the cream cheese. Seventh, we eat our snack!"

Building Understanding of Number Recognition

Recognizing the number symbols requires important skills. Children must be able to recognize numbers that are the same or different, recognize that the number represents a specific number of objects, and identify the number words: *one*, *two*, *three*, and so on. You can support children's understanding by providing a variety of materials with numbers on them:

- Wooden and magnetic numbers
- Number puzzles
- Foam number mats
- Dice numbered 1–9
- Variety of small counters

Separate each type of material into two groups: materials with the numbers from 0 to 4 and materials with numbers from 5 to 9. This will avoid confusion with too many numbers. Organize the materials in containers, and label each container. Place the containers on open shelving in the math area.

Children in Kaya's family home child care were engaged in number recognition activities. She encouraged them to find the materials, take them to an area to work in, and engage in an activity of their choosing. Kaya observed these activities and interacted with the children, depending on what they were doing. Melanie had found the large plastic numbers stored in a labeled container of numbers from 5 to 9. She brought these to a table and started to match the number 9.

Kaya: Do you know what number you're matching?

Melanie nodded.

Kaya: Why are you matching that number?

Melanie: I kind of get confused with the number 6 and the number 9. See, if you turn it upside down, it becomes a six.

Kaya also noticed that Aly-Muhammad was matching foam numbers to the numbers on a mat. Kaya knew that he was still learning to identify the numbers by name.

Kaya: Wow! You're doing a good job of matching the numbers. (pointing to each number) You matched the numbers 8, 7, and 3.

Aly-Muhammad beamed.

Roll and Match the Number

Materials

Numbered die

Mat with numbers 1-6 on it

Numbered blocks

What to Do

Set out the die, a mat with numbers on it, and numbered blocks.

Invite a child to roll the die and then find the block matching that number and put it on the correct number on his mat.

Learning in Action

Jamie rolled the die. It was a six. He found the six block and put it on the correct number on his mat. He again rolled his die and rolled another six. He quickly found another six block and placed it on top of the first six block on his mat. Kaya said, "Wow! You rolled and found two sixes. I like the way you placed one six on top of the other."

Twisty Numbers

Materials

Large, interlocking foam mats

Permanent marker

What to Do

Using the marker, write a number 0-10 on each mat.

To play the game, an adult (or one child) calls out a number. A child places a body part on the number called. Continue as long as the children are interested.

Building Understanding of Object Counting

Counting should start with the number zero, so that the children have a clear understanding of where the number zero fits into the numbering system and the importance of zero. As children's skills develop, offer opportunities to practice counting from a number other than zero, such as five, and counting in the reverse direction as well. A multitude of materials is available to use for counting:

- Small cubes—wooden or foam of various colors
- Counters
- Linear mats of various lengths
- Unit cubes

Small blocks are a good choice as they are easy to move and align both horizontally and vertically. Horizontal alignments make counting easy because children can move the blocks easily as they count them.

> Jackson decided to use the unit cubes to create two sets. He connected and counted five cubes and then created a second set and compared them visually. He declared, "They are the same. You can see that they are the same."

Alicia had created an alignment of wooden cubes. As she counted them, she moved each block to one side. In this way, she was able to count the blocks accurately because she could readily see which blocks had been counted. She then decided to use the same blocks to create a vertical structure. As she built the structure, she counted each block she placed.

ALICIA: See? It's four too!

MS. MARLENA: Good for you. You made four things in two different ways. First, you lined four cubes up, and then you stacked the four cubes.

Once children are able to recognize numbers, start setting up additional activities to encourage matching number symbols to quantities. To support maximum independence and creativity, allow the children to choose:

- The materials they wish to work with
- Where they would like to work
- How long they wish to engage in a task
- How to document their activities: ask to have photographs taken, document their own progress

Mara lined up a number of small rocks in a horizontal arrangement. She counted the rocks by pointing to each one as she counted it.

Mara: See, I have six rocks.

Ms. Marlena: I see that. Could you do this a different way?

Mara thought about it and then nodded. She went to the math shelf and brought back three different mats and a container of fish.

Mara: I picked three mats. See? One is short, one is very long, and one is sort of medium. I'm going to see how many fish fit on each mat.

Mara counted the fish on each mat.

Mara: You can see which one has more and which one has less.

Marlena: Good for you. You've created four different sets, and they all have a different number of objects in them, except that one fish set was the same as your rock set.

Mara: Yeah, you're right. I forgot about the rocks.

Activities for Counting across the Curriculum

Many of the daily activities that children engage in lend themselves to counting experiences.

Art

Printmaking

Materials

Paper

Paint

Markers

Small cups

Items for making prints, such as blocks, clean flyswatters, seedpods, small branches, leaves, and so on

What to Do

Set out paper, markers, printmaking materials, and cups of paint in the art center. Encourage the children to explore the materials.

When a child creates a print several times across the paper, encourage her to count the number of prints and write that number on the paper with a marker.

Draw a Set

Materials

Large paper

Writing utensils, such as pencils, crayons, and markers

Materials to trace, such as tangrams, blocks, shapes, and so on

What to Do

Put the materials out on a table.

Encourage the children to choose an item to trace onto the paper or simply draw an object a number of times to create a set.

Encourage them to count the number of items they have in the set and to write that number next to the items.

Block Center

Materials

Blocks

What to Do

Blocks provide a natural activity for counting. As the children build their structures, ask them to count how many blocks high, wide, or long the structure is.

Encourage them to count how many blocks they have used in a structure in total.

Challenge Cards

Materials

Index cards

Markers

3-ring binder

Plastic sleeves

Camera

What to Do

Children enjoy challenges, especially when they can be a part of creating a challenge.

Help them create challenge cards to encourage each other to build things that are equal in number or have a certain number of blocks.

Place the challenge cards in a three-ring binder for the children to choose.

When a child completes a challenge, take a photograph and add it to the binder with the challenge card, so other children can see what structures have been created and what they might want to try.

Learning in Action

> **OLIVIA:** I first counted how many, then I made it exactly the same.
>
> **AYDEN:** I looked and looked. Then I made a harder challenge. It has fourteen blocks.

Carpentry

Materials

Wood

Nails

Screws

Screwdrivers

Hammers

What to Do

As the children engage with the materials in the center, ask them to count how many nails or screws are needed to hold things together or how many pieces of wood they used to create a structure.

Dramatic Play

Materials

Materials will vary depending on the children's interests

What to Do

There are so many counting opportunities in role-playing and imaginary play. For example:

- How many plates to you need to set the table?
- How many buttons will you need to fasten to put on the firefighter jacket?
- How many muffins should you cook for your bakery?

Incorporate counting into any dramatic play the children enjoy.

Library Center

Materials

Books that have items to count

What to Do

As the children explore the books, encourage them to count:

- items, people, or animals
- by color, shape, or size

See the resources list on pages 144–145 for more suggestions.

Science Center

Materials

Foam lily pads

Foam or plastic numbers

Frog or turtle counters

Container with water

What to Do

Fill a container with water, and float foam lily pads on the surface.

Encourage the children to place frog or turtle counters on the lily pads.

Encourage them to count the frogs or turtles and place the corresponding number on each lily pad.

Outdoor Play

Materials

Materials will vary

What to Do

As the children play, encourage them to count. For example, ask:

- How many steps must you take to get from here to the fence?
- How many bars can you climb on the climbing toy?
- How many times can you swing back and forth?
- How many times around the path can you ride the tricycle?
- How many times can you bounce the ball?

Activities for Counting

Clip and Match

Materials

Clothespins

Plastic bin

Construction paper

Marker

What to Do

Using a marker, write a number from zero to ten on sheets of construction paper (one number per sheet). Laminate the mats for durability, if desired.

Place these number mats and a bin of clothespins on a table.

Encourage the children to clip clothespins to each mat to equal the number in the center of the mat.

Cube Collector

Materials

55 or more small wooden or foam cubes

11 small clear jars or containers

Construction paper

Marker

Scissors

Clear contact paper or laminator

What to Do

On construction paper, trace the outline of the bottom of the jars to create eleven circles. Cut these out.

On each circle, write a number from zero to ten.

Place the circles in a grid arrangement on a large sheet of paper. Cover with contact paper or laminate for durability.

Put the mat, the containers, and a bin of cubes on a table.

Encourage the children to put a number of cubes in each container on top of the corresponding numeral.

Counter Match

Materials

Chart paper

Markers

Tape

Photo of something that interests the children

Counters to match the subject of the photo

What to Do

Print or cut out a photo of something the children are interested in, such as a car, a monkey, a bear, or an airplane. Tape the photo to the chart paper.

Put the chart paper, markers, and counters that match the subject of the photo on a table.

Encourage the children to place their own number of counters on the chart and to write the corresponding number symbol next to the counters. More than one child can do this on a chart paper.

Post the charts in the classroom when the children are finished with them.

Roll and Build

Materials

Die

Blocks

What to Do

Set out a die and blocks in the block area or another area where the children can build structures.

Encourage the children to roll the die and count the number of dots showing on top.

They then build a structure from the number of blocks that matches the number showing on the die.

Then they roll again, count the dots, and add that number of blocks to the existing structure.

Number Match

Materials

Placemat

Plastic numbers

Counters

Plastic bins

What to Do

Put the placemat on a table. Set out a bin of plastic numbers and a bin of counters.

Encourage the children to pull out a number and line up a corresponding number of counters.

Tangram Counting

Materials

Tangram pieces

Mat

What to Do

Place the tangrams and mat on a table.

Encourage the children to make whatever they like out of the tangrams. When they make something, encourage them to count the number of tangrams they used.

Learning in Action

> **Mr. Andrew:** Chloe, can you tell me about what you're doing?
>
> **Chloe:** They both have one hexagon and six diamonds, see? One has two orange squares and that makes him a boy. One has a square and one trapezoid and one triangle and that makes it a girl. They both have nine pieces. The boy and girl together are eighteen pieces.

Counting Cups

Materials

12-cup muffin tin

Permanent marker

Label stickers

Small counters

What to Do

On the bottom of each cup in the muffin tin, use the marker to write a number between zero and ten and the corresponding number word. (Note: One cup will be empty.)

Below each cup, place a label sticker and draw the corresponding number of dots on the label.

Encourage the children to count the dots and place the corresponding number of counters into the cups.

Hopscotch

Materials

Painter's tape (indoors)

Sidewalk chalk (outdoors)

What to Do

Using painter's tape, create a hopscotch game on the floor. In each box, tape a number from zero to ten. (Outdoors alternative: Use sidewalk chalk to create the hopscotch game.)

Vary the game from time to time by doing the following:

- Tape or write the numbers in reverse order (ten to zero).
- Tape or write the numbers starting from a number other than zero or one.

Encourage the children to hop or jump from one number to the next, reciting each number as they land on it.

Counting Beads

Materials

String or yarn

Masking tape

Beads for stringing

What to Do

Provide beads of various sizes, shapes, and colors.

Cut string or yarn in a variety of lengths, and wrap a piece of tape around each end to make stringing easier.

Encourage the children to string the beads. As they work, encourage them to count the number of beads they have strung on a length of yarn.

Post the bead strings in the classroom so children can count and recount beads.

Field Trips

Even field trips can be wonderful opportunities for counting. For example, on a field trip to a museum, the children were fascinated by the semiprecious rocks they saw there. Emma counted these in a variety of ways:

- My favorites—6
- White ones—4
- Clear ones—3

Conservation

One of the last skills to develop is *conservation of number*: the understanding that the number of objects counted remains constant even when the objects are spread out or are close together. As discussed in chapter 1, young children are easily influenced by what they see. So, to them, if it looks longer, then it *is* longer, and if it looks as if it has more objects, then it does. Even when a child is able to count objects, she may still insist that a set has more objects by the way it appears. To be successful with conservation number tasks, children need to have had the following experiences:

- Forming sets that are equal and unequal
- Using one-to-one correspondence strategies to count objects
- Implementing the sequence of numbers
- Understanding the last number counted represents the total quantity of the objects counted

Activities to Encourage Understanding of Number Conservation

Help children to understand that the number of objects counted does not change, by inviting them to participate in the following activities.

Comparing Sizes

Materials

Variety of found objects

What to Do

Engage the children in collecting items of different sizes from around the classroom or during outdoor play.

Ask them to order the objects by size. Talk about the meanings of *taller* and *wider*. This leads to understanding that size makes a difference when looking at things.

One-to-One Squares

Materials

8 ½" x 11" paper

Objects gathered from the classroom, such as counters, blocks, and so on

What to Do

Fold each piece of paper in half, and in half again, four times. Unfold the paper to reveal squares. Provide each child with a squared piece of paper.

Encourage the children to gather some objects from around the classroom and explore putting them in the squares, one per square. Let them experiment with putting objects of various sizes in the squares.

This activity develops the understanding that since every square has one piece in it, the number of objects on the paper squares is constant.

It's the Same Number

Materials

8 small objects, such as counters, blocks, and so on

Large mat

Linear mat

What to Do

Set out the small objects and the mats on a table.

Encourage the children to place the objects on the large mat and then count the objects.

Next, encourage them to rearrange the objects on the large mat and then count them again. The total number is the same!

Encourage the children to line the objects up on the linear mat and then count them again. This activity helps children understand that the number of objects stays the same, regardless of the arrangement.

For an extra challenge, do this activity with two sets of objects, and encourage the children to compare the two sets.

Counting Sets

Materials

Numeral tiles

Small objects, such as counters, blocks, and so on

What to Do

Place number tiles with multiples of the numbers zero to nine, along with small objects, such as counters, on a table.

Encourage the children to make linear sets of the objects.

Next, encourage them to count the number of objects in a line, placing a number tile underneath each object counted: 1 under the first object, 2 under the second, 3 under the third, and so on.

As children gain experience in forming sets and counting, conservation of number will gradually emerge.

Resources to Support Counting

Songs

Six Little Ducks

*Six little ducks that I once knew
Fat ones, skinny ones, fair ones too
But the one little duck with the feather on his back
He led the others with his quack, quack, quack*

*A quack quack quack. A quack quack quack.
He led the others with his quack, quack, quack.*

*Down to the river they would go,
A wibble wobble, wibble wobble, to and fro.
But the one little duck with the feather on his back,
He led the others with a quack quack quack.*

*A quack quack quack. A quack quack quack.
He led the others with a quack quack quack.*

*Home from the river they would come,
A wibble wobble, wibble wobble, ho hum hum.
But the one little duck with the feather on his back,
He led the others with a quack quack quack.*

*A quack quack quack. A quack quack quack.
He led the others with a quack quack quack.
A quack quack quack quack—
QUACK QUACK!*

Five Green and Speckled Frogs

Five green and speckled frogs (**Hold five fingers on top of your other arm**)
Sat on a speckled log
Eating the most delicious bugs. Yum! Yum!
One jumped into the pool (**Jump a finger off your arm**)
Where it was nice and cool
Now there are four green and speckled frogs (**Hold up four fingers**)

Four green and speckled frogs (**Hold four fingers on top of your other arm**)
Sat on a speckled log
Eating the most delicious bugs. Yum! Yum!
One jumped into the pool (**Jump a finger off your arm**)
Where it was nice and cool
Now there are three green and speckled frogs (**Hold up three fingers**)

Three green and speckled frogs (**Hold three fingers on top of your other arm**)
Sat on a speckled log
Eating the most delicious bugs. Yum! Yum!
One jumped into the pool (**Jump a finger off your arm**)
Where it was nice and cool
Now there are two green and speckled frogs (**Hold up two fingers**)

Two green and speckled frogs (**Hold two fingers on top of your other arm**)
Sat on a speckled log
Eating the most delicious bugs. Yum! Yum!
One jumped into the pool (**Jump a finger off your arm**)
Where it was nice and cool
Now there is one green and speckled frog (**Hold up one finger**)

One green and speckled frog (**Hold one finger on top of your other arm**)
Sat on a speckled log
Eating the most delicious bugs. Yum! Yum!
It jumped into the pool (**Jump a finger off your arm**)
Where it was nice and cool
Now there are no more speckled frogs!

The Ants Go Marching

The ants go marching one by one, hurrah, hurrah!
The ants go marching one by one, hurrah, hurrah!
The ants go marching one by one
The little one stops to suck his thumb
And they all go marching down to the ground
To get out of the rain, BOOM! BOOM! BOOM! BOOM!

The ants go marching two by two, hurrah, hurrah!
The ants go marching two by two, hurrah, hurrah!
The ants go marching two by two
The little one stops to tie his shoe
And they all go marching down to the ground
To get out of the rain, BOOM! BOOM! BOOM! BOOM!

The ants go marching three by three, hurrah, hurrah!
The ants go marching three by three, hurrah, hurrah!
The ants go marching three by three
The little one stops to climb a tree
And they all go marching down to the ground
To get out of the rain, BOOM! BOOM! BOOM! BOOM!

The ants go marching four by four, hurrah, hurrah!
The ants go marching four by four, hurrah, hurrah!
The ants go marching four by four
The little one stops to shut the door
And they all go marching down to the ground
To get out of the rain, BOOM! BOOM! BOOM! BOOM!

The ants go marching five by five, hurrah, hurrah!
The ants go marching five by five, hurrah, hurrah!
The ants go marching five by five
The little one stops to take a dive
And they all go marching down to the ground
To get out of the rain, BOOM! BOOM! BOOM! BOOM!

The ants go marching six by six, hurrah, hurrah!
The ants go marching six by six, hurrah, hurrah!
The ants go marching six by six
The little one stops to pick up sticks
And they all go marching down to the ground
To get out of the rain, BOOM! BOOM! BOOM! BOOM!

(continued on next page)

(continued from previous page)

The ants go marching seven by seven, hurrah, hurrah!
The ants go marching seven by seven, hurrah, hurrah!
The ants go marching seven by seven
The little one stops to pray to heaven
And they all go marching down to the ground
To get out of the rain, BOOM! BOOM! BOOM! BOOM!

The ants go marching eight by eight, hurrah, hurrah!
The ants go marching eight by eight, hurrah, hurrah!
The ants go marching eight by eight
The little one stops to roller skate
And they all go marching down to the ground
To get out of the rain, BOOM! BOOM! BOOM! BOOM!

The ants go marching nine by nine, hurrah, hurrah!
The ants go marching nine by nine, hurrah, hurrah!
The ants go marching nine by nine
The little one stops to check the time
And they all go marching down to the ground
To get out of the rain, BOOM! BOOM! BOOM! BOOM!

The ants go marching ten by ten, hurrah, hurrah!
The ants go marching ten by ten, hurrah, hurrah!
The ants go marching ten by ten
The little one stops to shout, "The End!"
And they all go marching down to the ground
To get out of the rain.

Ten in a Bed

There were ten in a bed
And the little one said,
"Roll over! Roll over!"
So they all rolled over and one fell out

There were nine in the bed
And the little one said,
"Roll over! Roll over!"
So they all rolled over and one fell out

There were eight in the bed
And the little one said,
"Roll over! Roll over!"
So they all rolled over and one fell out

There were seven in the bed
And the little one said,
"Roll over! Roll over!"
So they all rolled over and one fell out

There were six in the bed
And the little one said,
"Roll over! Roll over!"
So they all rolled over and one fell out

There were five in the bed
And the little one said,
"Roll over! Roll over!"
So they all rolled over and one fell out

There were four in the bed
And the little one said,
"Roll over! Roll over!"
So they all rolled over and one fell out

There were three in the bed
And the little one said,
"Roll over! Roll over!"
So they all rolled over and one fell out

There were two in the bed
And the little one said,
"Roll over! Roll over!"
They both rolled over and one fell out

There was one in the bed
And the little one said,
"Peace at last!"

Hickory Dickory Dock

Hickory dickory dock
The mouse ran up the clock
The clock struck one.
The mouse ran down.
Hickory dickory dock

Hickory dickory dock
The snake crawled up the clock
The clock struck two.
The snake crawled down.
Hickory dickory dock

Hickory dickory dock
The squirrel climbed up the clock
The clock struck three.
The squirrel climbed down.
Hickory dickory dock

Hickory dickory dock
The cat ran up the clock.
The clock struck four.
The cat ran down.
Hickory dickory dock

Hickory dickory dock
The monkey climbed up the clock
The clock struck five.
The monkey climbed down.
Hickory dickory dock

Hickory dickory dock
The elephant went up the clock.
Oh no!
Hickory dickory dock

Rhymes

Five Currant Buns

*Five currant buns in the baker's shop,
Big and round with a cherry on top.
Along came Mary with a penny one day,
Bought a currant bun and took it away.*

*Four currant buns in the baker's shop,
Big and round with a cherry on top.
Along came Betty with a penny one day,
Bought a currant bun and took it away.*

*Three currant buns in the baker's shop,
Big and round with a cherry on top.
Along came Jack with a penny one day,
Bought a currant bun and took it away.*

*Two currant buns in the baker's shop,
Big and round with a cherry on top.
Along came John with a penny one day,
Bought a currant bun and took it away.*

*One currant bun in the baker's shop,
Big and round with a cherry on top.
Along came Jan with a penny one day,
Bought a currant bun and took it away.*

*No currant buns in the baker's shop,
Nothing big and round with a cherry on top.
Along came Ben with a penny one day,
"Sorry," said the baker, "no more currant buns today!"*

Five Little Monkeys

Five little monkeys jumping on the bed
One fell off and bumped his head.
Mama called the doctor and the doctor said,
"No more monkeys jumping on the bed!"

Four little monkeys jumping on the bed
One fell off and bumped his head.
Mama called the doctor and the doctor said,
"No more monkeys jumping on the bed!"

Three little monkeys jumping on the bed
One fell off and bumped his head.
Mama called the doctor and the doctor said,
"No more monkeys jumping on the bed!"

Two little monkeys jumping on the bed
One fell off and bumped his head.
Mama called the doctor and the doctor said,
"No more monkeys jumping on the bed!"

One little monkey jumping on the bed
He fell off and bumped his head.
Mama called the doctor and the doctor said,
"Put those monkeys right to bed!"

One, Two, Buckle My Shoe

One, two, buckle my shoe
Three, four, shut the door
Five, six, pick up sticks
Seven, eight, lay them straight
Nine, ten, begin again

One Potato, Two Potatoes

One potato, two potatoes, three potatoes, four,
Five potatoes, six potatoes, seven potatoes, more.
Eight potatoes, nine potatoes, ten potatoes, all.
One, two, three, four, five, six, seven, eight, nine, ten.

Ten Fat Sausages

Ten fat sausages sizzling in a pan,
Ten fat sausages sizzling in a pan,
One went pop and the other went bang!
Now there's eight fat sausages sizzling in a pan.

Eight fat sausages sizzling in a pan,
Eight fat sausages sizzling in a pan,
One went pop and the other went bang!
Now there's six fat sausages sizzling in a pan.

Six fat sausages sizzling in a pan
Six fat sausages sizzling in a pan
One went pop and the other went bang!
Now there's four fat sausages sizzling in a pan.

Four fat sausages sizzling in a pan,
Four fat sausages sizzling in a pan,
One went pop and the other went bang!
Now there's two fat sausages sizzling in a pan.

Two fat sausages sizzling in a pan,
Two fat sausages sizzling in a pan,
One went pop and the other went bang!
Now there's no fat sausages sizzling in a pan.

No fat sausages sizzling in a pan,
No fat sausages sizzling in a pan,
Ten went bang, bang, bang, bang!
Now there's no fat sausages sizzling in a pan.

Five Little Ducks

Five little ducks went out one day
Over the hill and far away.
Mother duck said, "Quack, quack, quack, quack."
But only four little ducks came back.

Four little ducks went out one day
Over the hill and far away.
Mother duck said, "Quack, quack, quack, quack,"
But only three little ducks came back.

Three little ducks went out one day
Over the hill and far away.
Mother duck said, "Quack, quack, quack, quack,"
But only two little ducks came back.

Two little ducks went out one day
Over the hill and far away.
Mother duck said, "Quack, quack, quack, quack,"
But only one little duck came back.

One little duck went out one day
Over the hill and far away.
Mother duck said, "Quack, quack, quack, quack,"
And all of the little ducks came back.

Books

Carle, Eric. 1968/1987. *1, 2, 3 to the Zoo: A Counting Book.* Syracuse, NY: Simon and Schuster.

Gerber, Carole. 2016. *10 Busy Brooms.* New York: Random House.

Scarry, Richard. 2010. *Richard Scarry's Best Counting Book Ever.* New York: Penguin Random House.

Seuss, Dr., as Theo LeSieg. 1961. *Ten Apples Up on Top!* New York: Random House.

Walsh, Ellen Stoll. 1995. *Mouse Count.* New York: HMH Books for Young Readers.

Wick, Walter, and Jean Marzollo. 1996. *I Spy Spooky Night: A Book of Picture Riddles.* New York: Scholastic.

Yaccarino, Dan. 2018. *Five Little Pumpkins Came Back.* New York: HarperCollins.

Chapter Summary

The ability to object count affects a great number of additional math skills, including measurement, computations, and effective problem solving. Encourage children to succeed by giving them opportunities that provide interesting and realistic challenges, support their developmental levels, engage them in active participation, develop independence, and develop positive attitudes toward lifelong learning.

Apply the Learning

1. You notice that when one of the children counts, she is not able to tell you how many she has counted. How could you explain this? What strategies might you use to help her to object count?

2. What strategies might you use to encourage object counting during daily routines? Identify the routine and the strategies you would use.

3. What strategies might you use to encourage support for object counting at home?
   - What methods might you use to explain the importance of object counting to families?
   - What strategies might you encourage family members to use?

4. During outdoor play, how might you encourage object counting while the children use the climbing equipment, play in the sand area, and ride trikes or other mobile equipment?

CHAPTER 06

Patterning

"Patterning is fundamental to mathematics and serves as the cornerstone of algebraic thinking. Early childhood patterning skills include being able to recognize, extend, create, and copy patterns."

—Angela Eckhoff,
Creative Investigations in Early Math

Patterning Defined

Juliet Robertson, author of *Messy Maths* (2017), defines *patterns* as "repeating sequences or arrangements of objects, numbers, actions, and events that systematically follow a given rule." Patterning is essential in developing mathematical thinking. Through patterning activities, children develop spatial awareness; skills in counting, sequencing, and ordering; mathematical reasoning; and the ability to make comparisons.

Patterning affects every phase of our lives. Patterns are all around us, in nature; in our architecture; in music, sports, communication, art, and dance; and in acquiring most of our academic skills. For the early years, we will consider the following types of patterns:

- **Attribute patterns:** patterns created by attributes such as color, shape, or size
- **Number patterns:** involve manipulating a sequence of numbers and objects to form patterns, such as two apples, three apples, two apples, three apples; also includes skip counting by twos, fives, and tens.
- **Line patterns:** a series of lines or shapes repeated regularly across a page

Patterns in Nature

Participating in outdoor activities is an important aspect of normal development. Outdoor activities, including field trips, provide opportunities to transfer learning from indoor to outdoor environments, and vice versa. Children can engage in outdoor patterning activities in many ways.

For example, they can observe and identify patterns, such as stripes and height. They can collect items and use them to create patterns. Children can make patterns of movement.

Carley decided to create some patterns on the monkey bars:

- "Left hand, right hand, left hand, right hand"
- "One hand up, one hand down, one hand up, one hand down"
- "Legs bent, legs straight, legs bent, legs straight"

Ages and Stages of Patterning

The ages and stages at which children recognize and can extend or create patterns very much depend on their background experiences.

Chapter 6: Patterning

Table 6.1: Ages and Stages of Patterning

AGE	SKILLS AND ABILITIES
Three to four years old	• Recognizes a simple pattern • Verbalizes a pattern while looking at it
Four to five years old	• Fills in a missing element of a pattern • Duplicates simple one-attribute patterns • Extends or fills in simple one-attribute patterns • Begins to initiate building simple one-attribute patterns • Names a pattern by one attribute
Five to six years old	• Extends and creates patterns with • more than one attribute • Names patterns by more than one • attribute

(Clements and Sarama, 2009; Robertson, 2017)

Jenna had started a color pattern and left it on the table. Six-year-old Jusef saw it there and copied the pattern, and then he extended it.

Jusef: Red hat with yellow shirt and blue pants, yellow hair with green shirt and blue pants. It's a people pattern!

Kaylee: Look! Purple bear, yellow bear, purple bear, yellow bear.

Davina: I made a complicated pattern. It's by number and by color and by size. See? Three long blue rectangles and one short green rectangle.

The Facilitator's Role

The major role of the facilitator is to observe the children and provide the appropriate materials to encourage the various levels of skills and abilities, occasionally adding and changing materials that are of current interest to the children. Use vocabulary to describe the patterns you see, and encourage the children to use these words, too: *after, again, repeated, on and on, before, next to, above, over, below, under, curved, straight, in between, in and out, different, same, spiral, spotted, striped, zigzag, up, down*.

Capitalize on patterning opportunities across daily routines. For example, invite the children to line up in a pattern, such as by gender, color of clothes, sitting and standing, length of hair, and so on. At mealtimes, provide patterned napkins, or provide napkins in different colors and encourage the children to put them out in a pattern. Invite the children to create placemats using strips of colored paper to weave into a pattern. Ask the children what patterns they can find, such as eating red fruits and green vegetables for snack: red, green, red, green. Invite the children to wear a pattern to school and to describe it.

Documenting Patterning

Documentation is important because it provides valuable information to help adults provide the appropriate materials to enhance learning, encourage practice of emergent skills, and know what the next steps in the child's learning should be. The best documentation techniques are those you can use in more than one setting.

Observations should be made at different times and in different settings. We'll take a look at a few ways to observe and document patterning:

- Skill chart
- Graph
- Rubric
- Documentation panel

Skill Chart

When you observe a child creating a pattern, record the date and any relevant comments. To qualify as having mastered a type of pattern, you should observe the child creating that type of pattern at least three times in three different settings. You can put this type of documentation into a child's portfolio and use it to report progress to family members.

Sample Patterning Skill Chart

Name: Jamie

DATE	COMMENTS
10/14/2020	Patterned leaves by size and color
10/15/2020	Patterned farm animals by size and color

Graph

Children can and will document their own progress. Create a simple graph to let them color in the blocks for patterning skills, such as patterning by color, shape, size, and number. For example, in this prekindergarten class, the children could choose from activities during the regular math period each day. Their teacher simply told them that it was patterning time. The children chose their own materials and gathered their own graphs. They worked on the skills that they had yet to accomplish. They could also work on their graphs during other times of the day.

Kelly knew how to use a graph because her teacher had previously taught and reinforced this skill. She knew she had to record her activity at least three times and that an adult had to verify her documentation. Kelly was very proud of her accomplishment, as she had completed all the expectations for patterning for this graph. She promptly shared her success with her mother at dismissal time. Her teacher put the graph into Kelly's portfolio, along with her rubric and photos of her work, as validation of her learning.

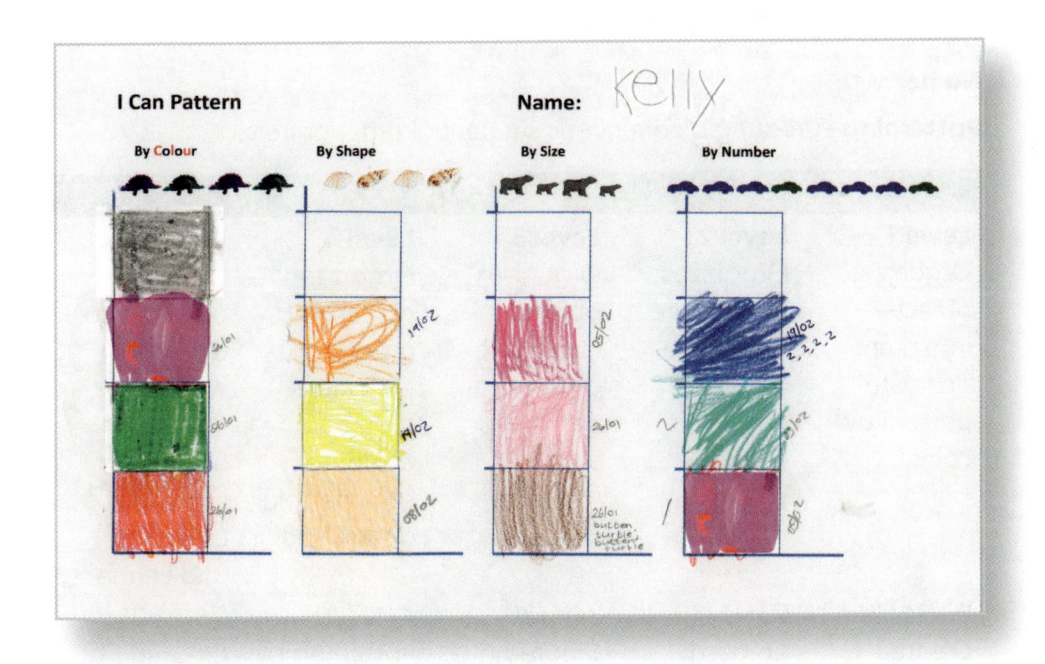

Rubric

A rubric is probably the most efficient and time-saving method of documenting learning. A rubric gives accurate information in a timely fashion with no need for formal periodic assessment and can be easily kept in a child's portfolio. You can use a rubric to report to parents on an ongoing basis, and if the rubrics are centrally stored, families can look at them to check their child's progress. If you digitize rubrics, you can post a child's progress on the family's secure portal.

In this example, the bar at the top of each skill level is colored green when the child has mastered that skill. When she has mastered a skill that is advanced for her age, that bar is colored blue.

A bar would be colored red, or simply left blank, to indicate that more work is needed on a particular skill. Attach any supporting photos to the rubric.

Sample Patterning Rubric

Name: Mia

Patterning—Creating a continuous sequential order of items

Level 1 Organizes objects into a one-attribute pattern by color	Level 2 Organizes objects into a one-attribute pattern by shape	Level 3 Organizes objects into a one-attribute pattern by size	Level 4 Organizes objects into a pattern with more than one attribute, such as color and shape	Level 5 Organizes objects into a pattern with more than two attributes, such as color, size, and shape
03/16/20: Created pattern of blue and red blocks	03/16/20: Created pattern of triangle blocks and square blocks	3/16/20: Created pattern of large and small triangle blocks	4/18/20: Patterned by direction and color	06/19/20: Created pattern of butterflies of different color, type, and number

06/20/20: Created pattern by following template of direction, color, and design |

Comments:

04/18/20:

06/20/20:

Documentation Panel

A documentation panel is a display of artifacts, such as photographs, quotes, descriptions, and other items, that show children's understanding of a concept. It could be in the form of a bulletin board, a poster board, or a tabletop display. Develop documentation panels to share information with family members.

Patterns at the Zoo

On our trip to the zoo, we saw zebras. Zebras have a stripe pattern just like tigers. The children were fascinated when they learned that a baby zebra has brown stripes that change to black as it grows up.

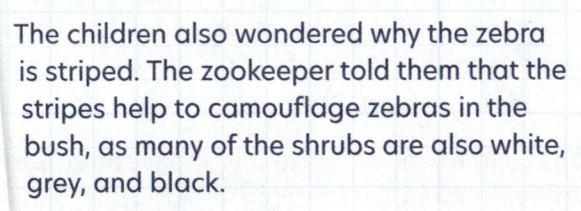

The children also wondered why the zebra is striped. The zookeeper told them that the stripes help to camouflage zebras in the bush, as many of the shrubs are also white, grey, and black.

Danny's Patterns

Danny: I made a size pattern.

Danny not only made a size pattern but also has learned to ignore other factors, such as color, in making a pattern.

Building Understanding of Patterning

With experiences in matching and one-to-one correspondence, copying a pattern is an easy task for children. Develop the associated vocabulary of patterning by modeling the words and asking children to use them as they create their patterns. Model and help the children develop understanding of types of patterns. Often, teachers describe patterns using alphabet letters, such as ABAB patterns. These descriptions have very little meaning to a young child who has not yet learned alphabet letters or how to transfer that learning to patterning, because they involve more than two attributes at a time. Instead, help the children relate to the type of pattern created—color, shape, size, or number.

Provide appropriate resources to help maintain children's interest and diversify learning: books, photographs, and items added to classroom collections by families. Build interest and experience by going on field trips and inviting expert visitors to the classroom.

Encourage children to recognize and label patterns around them, both indoors and outdoors. Go for a patterning walk, and talk about all the patterns you observe, such as brickwork in a building, the colors on a bulletin board, flowers and other plants, and feathers on a bird. Take photographs of the patterns, and post them along with the children's comments in the classroom, where the children can review and reflect on them over time. Keep the display open ended to encourage families to become involved and add items they find at home.

The children noticed two patterns in the outdoor playground.

MANDY: The pots are black, white, black, white. It's a color pattern.

JOSHUA: There's a plant in one tire, no plant in the next one, then another plant and no plant in the last one. It's sort of a number pattern, none and one.

Chandra brought in a photo of her dad's workplace.

CHANDRA: A yellow crane, then a white crane, then a yellow crane, then a white one. It's a color pattern.

Marcia made a word pattern.

MARCIA: I used picture cards and word cards to make my pattern.

Chapter 6: Patterning

Invite the children to engage in activities that promote patterning, such as the following:

- Walk around the room to the beat of a drum: one foot, the other foot, one foot, the other foot.
- Touch body parts in order: head, shoulders, head, shoulders.
- Play games such as Duck, Duck, Goose.
- Create a footprint pattern to follow as they move around the room.

Organizing Materials

Almost any materials are appropriate for patterning. How you organize the materials will encourage the children to create patterns. As discussed in chapter 2, take an *intentional learning approach* based on the emergent skills and the behaviors of the children. They need to practice emergent skills, and not all children are at the same level of skill development. Reflect on the skills you want to support in the children, and provide materials that will help them develop those skills.

Patterning by One Attribute

Materials

Linear strip mats

String

Containers

Beads, counters, buttons, and so on

What to Do

When there is only one difference in color, size, or shape, the children are less likely to get confused or distracted by too many options. Organize the materials by a single attribute. For example, to encourage the children to focus on size, offer different containers holding items in the same color and shape, but with each containing only one size: small red stars or large red stars.

To help the children focus on shape, offer different containers holding items of the same color and size, but with each containing only one shape, such as small green beads or small green buttons.

To help them focus on color, fill containers with materials in two different colors that have the same size and shape. For example, provide string and two containers of small beads in green and yellow.

Patterning by Two Attributes

Materials

Linear strip mats

String

Containers

Beads, counters, buttons, and so on

What to Do

Organize the materials in different containers. This type of strategy adds an extra dimension to children's learning because they have to plan which type of pattern they want to complete, then gather the required materials. They could create patterns by color, size, shape, or number.

Alternatively, containers could hold a mixture of objects such as objects of different sizes and colors but the same shape: for example, large and small bear counters in red and blue. Or containers could hold items of different colors and shapes but the same size, such as green and yellow counters shaped like bears and stars, all of them small. Containers could hold items of different shapes and sizes but the same color, such as blue counters in large and small bears and stars. Either strategy will work but is dependent on the learner. Some learners are more independent and relish the opportunity to plan what they wish to accomplish.

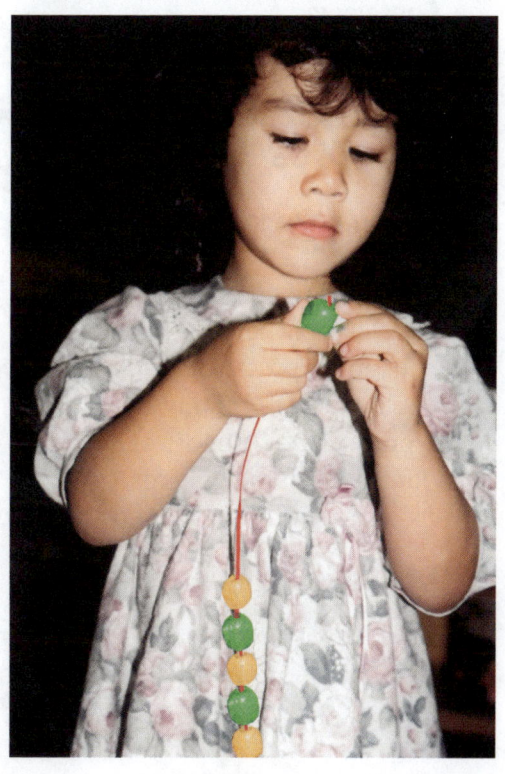

Learning in Action

Martin collected some blocks and a large white folded paper.

Martin: My pattern is a number and shape pattern. One, two, one, two, one, and butterfly shape and triangles.

Haeran: My pattern is a color and a sit-down and stand-up pattern.

Patterning by More than Two Attributes

Materials

Linear strip mats

String

Containers

Beads, counters, buttons, and so on

What to Do

The organization for this type of patterning is more open ended as children have established the concept of patterning. You could store the materials by type, such as all bears of different colors and sizes, or all dinosaurs of different types, colors, and sizes.

Learning in Action

Danny explained, "I made a size pattern, big bears and small bears, and a two-color pattern. The little bears are green and purple. It's also a number pattern, one and two."

Patterning with Lines

Forming different arrangements with lines gives children experiences in seeing different perspectives. To help them gain understanding of lines, support the children in using vocabulary to describe various types of lines.

Ajay: I pasted vertical and horizontal lines on my paper. The vertical lines are up and down. The horizontal lines are from side to side.

Chloe: I pasted my lines to make triangles. They have two diagonal lines and one horizontal line.

Anton: I like making zigzag lines. They're cool.

Ajay: I made a whole bunch of circles and loops. I also made a vertical line with a little horizontal line on it.

Single Line Patterns

Materials
Scrap paper

Scissors

Glue

Paper

Small colored sticks or craft sticks

Straws in a variety of colors and lengths

Playdough

Crayons, pencils, markers

Paint and paintbrushes

Chapter 6: Patterning

What to Do

Provide large pieces of paper, glue, and materials that the children can cut, paint, or color and then arrange into line patterns. Some children will want to cut their own lines out of paper. Others will prefer to paint lines, glue craft sticks, or draw lines on paper.

Geometric Shape Patterns

Materials

Tangrams

Clear plastic geometric shapes

Plastic, foam, or wooden geometric shapes

Small colored sticks or craft sticks

Straws in a variety of colors and lengths

What to Do

Provide a variety of geometric shapes, and encourage the children to create patterns. Ask them to describe the patterns they make.

Activities for Patterning across the Curriculum

Provide materials, and let the children choose which materials they wish to use and which area they wish to work in. Patterning activities can take place in almost all areas of the curriculum.

Art

Print Patterns

Materials

Variety of paper, such as construction, newsprint, and sandpaper

Craft sticks

Small sticks

Paint in variety of colors and thicknesses

Items for making prints, such as blocks, clean flyswatters, stamps, and so on

Paintbrushes

Glitter

Markers, pencils, crayons, pastels

Pictures

Stickers

Scissors

Glue

Playdough

Plastic cookie cutters

What to Do

Set out a variety of materials, and encourage the children to create patterns. Note: You don't have to set out all the materials at once. Rotate them to keep the children's interest.

As they work, ask them to talk about the patterns they are making.

Learning in Action

Mya stated, "I made my pawprints twice. I have a color and shape pattern."

Block Center

Block Patterns

Materials

Large and small unit blocks, both plain and colored

Foam blocks

Design blocks

Duplo and Lego blocks

Bristle blocks

People figures

Traffic signs

Toy vehicles

Animal figures

What to Do

Set out the materials, and encourage the children to create patterns.

As they work, ask them to talk about the patterns they are making.

Take photos of the patterns and post them in the block area, or put them in a photo album for the children to review.

Dramatic Play

Pattern Dress-Up

Materials

Dress-up clothes

What to Do

Put the clothes in the dramatic play center. Encourage the children to get dressed in patterns. For example, one child puts a hat on, and the other does not, then a third child puts a hat on, and the fourth child does not.

Let the children decide on a new pattern.

Library Center

Pattern Ideas

Materials

Books with patterns

What to Do

With the children, read a book that incorporates patterns. (See the list on page 172 for suggestions.)

Talk with the children about the types of patterns they notice in the book.

Ask them to compare the similarities and differences of the patterns they see.

Talk about places where they might find the patterns.

Discuss with them how to make these patterns.

Music

We've Got Rhythm

Materials

Rhythm sticks

Drums

MP3 player

Variety of music

What to Do

Music is a natural way to support children in recognizing and repeating patterns. Play a song, and encourage the children to clap or stomp or use rhythm sticks to the rhythm of the notes or words they hear.

Try clapping or beating a drum to the rhythm of a known song and encourage the children to guess what song it is.

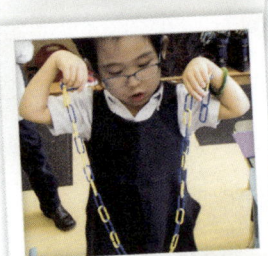

Manipulatives

Make a Pattern

Materials

Pegs and pegboards
Beads and beading string
Buttons
Pop beads
Clothespins
Plastic clips
Unit cubes
Small stacking cups
Small cubes
Tiles with photos of animals or other objects
Containers
Labels

What to Do

Provide a variety of materials in different colors, sizes, and shapes. Store the materials in labeled containers on labeled open shelves. Consider the levels of your group, and limit the materials if you think that some of the children will be overwhelmed by too many choices.

Encourage the children to create patterns and to describe the patterns they make.

Sand Area

Sand Tracks

Materials

Colored sand
Wet sand
Molding toys

What to Do

Invite the children to create tracks in the sand.

Encourage them to make prints with the molds in wet sand.

Encourage them to describe the patterns they create.

Science

Drip Patterns

Materials

Food coloring

Paper towels

What to Do

Provide food coloring and paper towels. Invite the children to make patterns of food-coloring drops on the paper towels.

Encourage them to describe the patterns they create.

Magnetic Patterns

Materials

Magnetic animals, vehicles, dinosaurs, and so on

Magnetic board or surface

What to Do

Put out the magnetic animals or vehicles and the magnetic board. Invite the children to make patterns with the magnets.

Encourage them to describe the patterns they create.

Activities for Finding Patterns in Nature

Natural patterns are everywhere. The patterns found in nature that are relevant for young children to understand and observe include symmetry, fractals, spirals, and spots and stripes.

- **Symmetry:** Symmetry exists when different sides of something are alike. For example, the two sides of a butterfly are exactly the same; this is called *bilateral symmetry*. Consider a starfish. No matter how you rotate it, it still looks the same.
- **Fractals:** *Fractals* are patterns that repeat indefinitely without changing the basic structure. This is an easy pattern for children to learn about as they see these patterns in a set of stairs, trees, leaves, lightning, or snowflakes. For example, when a leaf is small, just starting to grow, it will continue to form the same pattern and will look the same when it is fully grown.
- **Spirals:** A *spiral*, a curved pattern beginning from a central point, is also a common pattern in nature. Spirals are found in shells, sheep horns, pine cones, pineapples, and hurricanes. You can also see spirals in how leaves grow on the stem of a plant.
- **Spots and stripes:** Spots and stripes, such as the stripes on a tiger or zebra or the spots on a ladybug, lizard, or leopard, are common in the animal world.

Investigate the opportunities in your area for getting the children outside to explore the natural world. For example, you may be able to take a field trip to a local garden center or horticultural center, a wooded area or forest, or a public park. There may be beaches, rivers, or ponds where you can explore. A natural history museum, aquarium, or zoo would be a wonderful place to visit. Or you could simply take a walk around the neighborhood.

Before You Go

Identify the types of patterns the children can discover. For example, at a zoo or aquarium, they are likely to see spots and stripes on a variety of animals. At a natural history museum or aquarium, they will have an opportunity to find spirals. In a garden center or park, they will likely see fractals. Of course, symmetry can be found almost anywhere.

Prepare the children for the trip. Read a book about what they might see, or present photographs of some of the patterns that they can expect to see. Discuss the types of patterns and ensure that the children know what to look for. Also, talk with them and with the adult chaperones about your expectations for the trip. Remind them to stay with their group (and tell them what to do if they get separated) and to be respectful of the animals, plants, and other features they see, and give them any other important information.

Find out about any rules that museums, parks, or other public areas have in place, such as discarding trash or recycling in proper containers, not touching animals or displays, and not damaging live plants. Talk with the children about these rules.

Consider providing children with a passport type of booklet or a checklist, so that they can identify what they should be looking for. Show them how to check off, stamp, sticker, or mark a pattern when they find it. Tell them that they should show an adult what they've found so they can talk about the pattern together, and so the adult can verify that the child has found that pattern.

Passport for a Zoo Trip

Gather paper and construction paper. Cut the paper in half width-wise, and fold a couple of sheets in half. Cut a piece of construction paper in half, and staple it to the folded pages as a cover. Inside, glue photos of the plants, animals, or structures where the children will be able to find different patterns. Let the children decorate the covers of their passports, and help them write their names as well.

During the Activity

Engage the children by pointing out interesting patterns, and ask them to point out patterns that they recognize. Take photographs of the children and the patterns they discover. Remind them to check off the patterns in their passports or on their checklists.

If you visit an outdoor area, such as a public park, beach, or woodland, encourage the children to gather found items, such as fallen leaves, twigs, pebbles, or shells. Remind them to leave animals, insects, and live plants alone. If they find a particularly interesting live creature, they can ask an adult to take a photograph of it.

After You Go

Talk with the children about what they saw on the trip. Reflect with them on what they have learned, and record their comments. Use the photos and any notes you have to prepare documentation for the children.

Invite them to create drawings of what they saw and learned. If they collected items from the trip, encourage them to create patterns. Collect more information from a variety of sources, such as the library, family members, or expert guests.

Use photos of the items children discovered to make photo cards. Encourage the children to create patterns of the cards. Also, create a book of patterns using the photos of items the children saw
or collected.

Ask the children how they would like to show what they have learned.

After a trip to the zoo and reading books about the jungle, the children decided to create a jungle scene in the reading corner. They came up with a plan and worked together, with help from their teachers, to bring their idea to life. Afterward, they talked about what they had created and the patterns found there.

Jeremy: We all made a jungle scene.

Julie: There's growing patterns—the trees. Look at the leaves.

Van: There's stripe patterns. Look at the tiger.

Jordan: I made a symmetry pattern. It's the butterfly.

Marla: The pillow has a leaf pattern.

Chapter 6: Patterning

When the children returned from an excursion to a local beach, they wanted to decorate the fence of their school to show that their school is near the ocean. The whole primary school helped to make a pattern of fish on their fence.

JERMAINE: It's a stripe pattern.

JULES: It's also a curved pattern.

Resources to Support Patterning

Books for Children

Bleiman, Andrew, and Chris Eastland. 2018. *Zig Zag ZooBorns!* San Diego, CA: Beach Lane Books.

Goldstone, Bruce. 2015. *I See a Pattern Here*. New York: Henry Holt.

Hesselberth, Joyce. 2020. *Pitter Pattern*. New York: HarperCollins.

Olson, Nathan. 2007. *Animal Patterns*. North Mankato, MN: Capstone.

Olson, Nathan. 2007. *City Patterns*. North Mankato, MN: Capstone.

Olson, Nathan 2007. *Food Patterns*. North Mankato, MN: Capstone.

Olson, Nathan 2007. *People Patterns*. North Mankato, MN: Capstone.

Olson, Nathan 2007. *Plant Patterns*. North Mankato, MN: Capstone.

Pluckrose, Henry. 1995. *Pattern*. New York: Watts Books.

Steffora, Tracey. 2011. *Patterns at the Museum*. Chicago, IL: Heinemann Library.

Swinburne, Stephen. 2002. *Lots and Lots of Zebra Stripes*. Honesdale, PA: Boyds Mills Press.

Books for Adults

Campbell, Sarah, and Richard Campbell. 2010. *Growing Patterns.* Honesdale, PA: Boyds Mills Press.

Ball, Philip. 2016. *Patterns in Nature: Why the Natural World Looks the Way It Does.* Chicago, IL: University of Chicago Press.

Chapter Summary

Patterning is an important skill to master, as "[m]ath is underpinned by patterns which can be seen all around us" (Robertson, 2017). Patterns affect competence not only in math but also in music, writing, reading, science, and social interactions. Incorporate learning about patterns in all subject areas across the curriculum to ensure future academic success.

Apply the Learning

1. When Alicia patterned, she started out with a color pattern then switched to a shape pattern. Explain the reason for this change in patterning. What strategies might you use to mitigate this problem?

2. Outdoor field trips are a wonderful way to discover patterns in nature. Explore your neighborhood, and identify the types of patterns children might encounter. Also, look at possible field-trip opportunities in the local community.

3. What strategies might you use to encourage children to understand the different kinds of patterns—shape, color, and size? Consider the following:
   - Documentation panels
   - Teachable moments
   - Organization of the patterning area

CHAPTER 07

Measurement

"Young children apply early concepts of measurement in many of their everyday activities. They compare sizes of toys and portions of food, their own height to another's, the weights of two pumpkins, and the lengths of toy trains. In exploring ways of comparing, they may use nonstandard measurement tools such as hands and fingers to estimate length, blocks or squares for area, and sand and water for capacity."

—Linda Platas, "Measuring Up! Measurement in the Preschool Classroom"

Measurement Defined

Measurement is an essential skill, used in many aspects of our lives such as cooking, building structures, sewing, crafts, art, carpentry, and science. Measurement activities include the ability to understand concepts of length, size, and capacity and require children to be able to use tools, such as small cubes of the same size, to measure different aspects of an object.

According to Robertson (2017), Briggs (2013), and Crowther (2018a), children need core measurement activities to explore and understand concepts such as the following:

- **The language associated with measurement:** Children need to understand the meaning of *measuring*, as well as words associated with size, quantity, and capacity.

> When Danny measured his playdough, he said, "It's really long. It's twenty-one cubes long."

- **Making comparisons between objects and the measurements made:** Children need practice in comparing objects, measuring objects, and comparing their measurements.

> Gabrielle put the chicks side by side to see which one was taller.

- **Learning to estimate:** With practice in measuring and comparing, children will develop the ability to estimate size, quantity, and capacity.

> Aaliyah thought that the distance from the table to the door was twenty footsteps. She measured the distance with her feet and concluded that she was not right. She said, "It actually only took fifteen steps. It's shorter than I thought."

- **The conservation of measurement:** This is the concept that the quantity or volume remains the same even if it is rearranged or put into a container of a different shape but holding the same quantity.

> Samia was measuring to see which cup held more water. She was surprised that they both held the same amount. She was sure that the taller one would hold more water. Samia is still confused by the appearance of the objects.

- **Measuring objects using nonstandard tools:** Children need lots of practice using all sorts of items to measure.

> Danny used unit cubes to measure his playdough, and Aaliyah used footsteps to measure distance.

Ages and Stages of Measurement

Table 7.1: Ages and Stages of Learning to Measure

AGE	SKILLS AND ABILITIES
Two to three years old	Awareness of attributes: identifying physical attributes of an object, such as corners, length, width, size, and capacity
Three to four years old	• Making direct comparisons: comparing two items to see which is longer, shorter, bigger, heavier, and so on • Making indirect comparisons: measuring with a string to compare two items to see which is longer, taller, wider, and so on
Four to five years old	Measuring using nonstandard units, such as small equally sized cubes, unit cubes, or glass pebbles; child counts the number of items to indicate length, width, size, or capacity
Five years old and older	Measuring with standard units, such as rulers or measuring tapes; depends on child's ability to read numbers and to identify markings on measuring tools

(Crowther, 2018c, and Robertson, 2017)

The Facilitator's Role

One of the critical roles for the facilitator is to increase children's awareness of measurement vocabulary. For example, use terms that children are unlikely to have heard before, such as *perimeter*, *volume*, and *area*. Awareness of the actual terminology helps children develop a good foundation for later math skills. Model and reinforce the children's understanding of terms such as the following:

- *Perimeter, area, circumference, volume*
- *Length, width, height, distance*
- *Full, empty, half full, half empty*
- *Level, packed, overflowing*
- Comparative words, such as *long, longer, longest* and *heavy, heavier, heaviest*

Provide opportunities for children to develop the ability to measure accurately. For example, reinforce the idea that nonstandard units of measurement, such as unit blocks, should be placed precisely end to end. Comment positively on children's efforts. For example, as Jeremy measured how far he had jumped, he carefully placed his feet toe to heel, being careful to make sure one foot was exactly in front of the other. His teacher commented, "Jeremy, I like the way you are walking toe to heel so precisely to measure your distance." Help the children to choose appropriate measuring tools. Talk with them about which types of measuring tools work best in different situations.

Ms. Whitley: Marlena, you did an excellent job of measuring the perimeter of your book. It looks just like an outline of your book.

Ms. Whitley (to the group): Which types of objects did you use to measure things?

Marlena: I used the glass pebbles to go around a book to measure the perimeter. When you took the book out, you could see the shape of the book.

Naijeer: I used sticks to measure the length of the triceratops, but it didn't work. The sticks kept falling off.

Heidi: I used the string to measure the circumference of my head.

Ms. Whitley: Marlena, why do you think the pebbles worked?

Marlena: They work 'cause you can go around things. You can measure the perimeter 'cause they're all the same. I used them to measure area. You could fill the whole book with pebbles.

Ms. Whitley: When do you think pebbles might not work so well?

Marlena: When you try to stack them. They're slippery and fall over.

Naijeer: Would not work on the triceratops. They'd fall off just like the sticks.

Ms. Whitley: Why do you think the sticks did not work?

Naijeer: They fall off. They're not bendy, so it's hard to measure when it's curvy.

Ms. Whitley: Heidi, why do you think the string worked?

Heidi: It's bendy so you can go around things. You can cut it so it's exact. You can make it stiff so you can keep it.

Provide mobile containers to encourage children to gather objects to take to where they want to measure things. Plastic baskets or caddies with handles, especially ones that are compartmentalized, work best. Children can sort what they need into the different sections of the containers. This has an added advantage as it encourages children to think about and plan their activities.

Provide standard measuring tools for children who are ready to use them, and help them to understand how to use these tools. Standard tools include rulers, measuring tapes, and measuring lines. These tools should have large numbers and a minimum number of subdividing lines.

Documenting Learning to Measure

There are a few ways to document children's emerging measurement skills, such as graphs, rubrics, skill charts, and photographs.

Graphs

Provide a personal math folder for each child. Inside, place graphs where each child can document her progress in developing the skill she's working on. When a child updates a graph, she can talk with her teacher about what she has done, and the teacher can validate her effort.

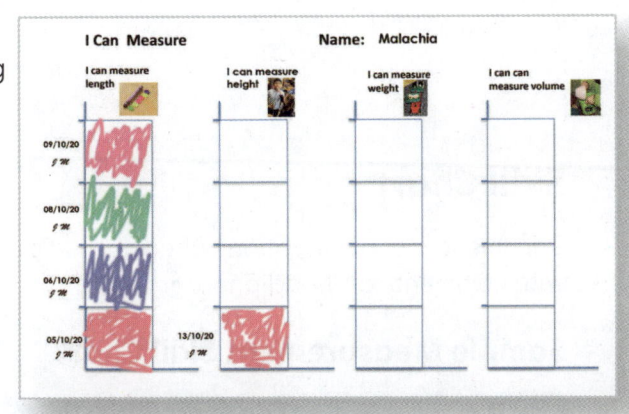

When you encourage children to document their own progress, they gain an understanding of what they know and what they still need to know, and they take pride in their personal achievements. They develop the ability to take charge of their own learning, and all have opportunities to create representations of their learning that are unique. They can share their experiences and perspectives with other children and the adults around them.

Chapter 7: Measurement

Rubrics

Enter the information from the child's self-evaluation graph directly into the rubric. When the measurement graph is completed, the graph can be placed behind the rubric in the child's math folder.

Sample Rubric for Measuring

Name: Malachia

LEVEL 1	LEVEL 2	LEVEL 3	LEVEL 4	LEVEL 5
Identifying physical attributes of an object: corners, length, width, size, and capacity	Making direct comparisons: comparing two items	Making indirect comparisons: comparing objects using items such as string	Measuring with nonstandard items, such as equally sized cubes See attached self-measure graph: length 4 x 09/10/20	Measuring with standard tools, such as rulers and measuring tapes

Skill Chart

Document your observations of each child's explorations. Fill in the chart with comments and add photographs as you observe the skills.

Sample Measurement Skill Chart

NAME	DATES	SKILL OBSERVED
Mason	8/10/20	Measured the perimeter of a block with unit cubes

Building Understanding of Measurement

Children engage in measurement activities at an early age, such as comparing sizes or quantities. They need to develop their understanding by using nonstandard units to measure familiar items, such as their heights, materials in their environments, or household objects. Dedicate a section of the math area to such materials as string, unit blocks, and other items, which the children can use for nonstandard measurements. Engage them in organizing the measurement area.

> The children in Miss Nelly's kindergarten class were very interested in measuring their heights. One of the children thought that using streamers would be a good way to measure, and all the children were excited to participate. When everyone had been measured, Miss Nelly helped them hang the streamers according to size on one wall of the classroom. The children actively engaged in conversation about who was the tallest, who was the shortest, who was in the middle, or who was second shortest.
>
> **Miss Nelly:** When you measured yourselves, why did you decide to use the streamer?
>
> **Nathan:** It's easy to use 'cause you can make it fit to anyone's height.
>
> **Damara:** You can hang them up and see how tall we are.
>
> **Jamie:** You can write your name on it and take it home.

Based on the children's interest, Miss Nelly decided to engage them in organizing a section of the math area for measuring.

Miss Nelly: What else could we measure?

Alayna: Just about everything—books, toys, the door, and just everything!

Aleksander: I want to measure my table and my books.

Nadia: Could we measure stuff like our heads and arms and legs?

Nash: How about some of the dishes and bowls?

Miss Nelly: What would we need to measure the things you talked about?

Alayna: Cubes and rectangles that are the same size, unit cubes, glass beads, pipe cleaners, straws with the connectors, Duplo cubes, paper rolls, the Tyrannosaurus rex 'cause they're all the same size.

Aleksander: String and yarn 'cause it has to go around things.

Nadia: Buttons that are the same size, little counting cups, the bears.

The children actively collected the materials and put them into the containers provided. Miss Nelly made signs for the containers and for the shelf, and the children decided how to organize the items on the shelf. In this way, they knew where the materials were and could engage in measurement activities, either during math time or during free play.

Activities for Measuring

Height

Materials

- Covered shoeboxes
- Children's whole body, feet, or hands
- Interlocking straws
- Hollow blocks
- Duplo blocks
- Small cubes of equal size
- Glass beads
- Counters
- Unit cubes
- Pompoms
- Buttons
- Little colored sticks
- String or rope

What to Do

Provide a variety of materials that the children can use to measure the height of furniture, each other, doors, and so on.

Safety note: If the children are using hollow blocks, supervise them closely to be sure that the structure they build is stable. Covered shoeboxes make excellent building materials and can be safely stacked higher than wooden blocks.

Learning in Action

Jivan: I am seven straws tall. I am taller than you. You are only six straws tall.

Joshua: High as me.

Kendal: It's taller than me.

Aly-Muhammad: I am measuring how high my drawing is.

Length

Materials

- Covered shoeboxes
- Children's whole body, feet, or hands
- Interlocking straws
- Hollow blocks
- Duplo blocks
- Small cubes of equal size
- Glass beads
- Counters
- Unit cubes
- Pompoms
- Buttons
- Little colored sticks
- String or rope

What to Do

Provide a variety of materials that the children can use to measure the length of items in the classroom.

Learning in Action

> **Miss Nelly:** What are you measuring?
>
> **Sophie:** How long baby is.
>
> **Kelsey:** Measuring how long our rope is.
>
> **Stephen:** How far I jumped.

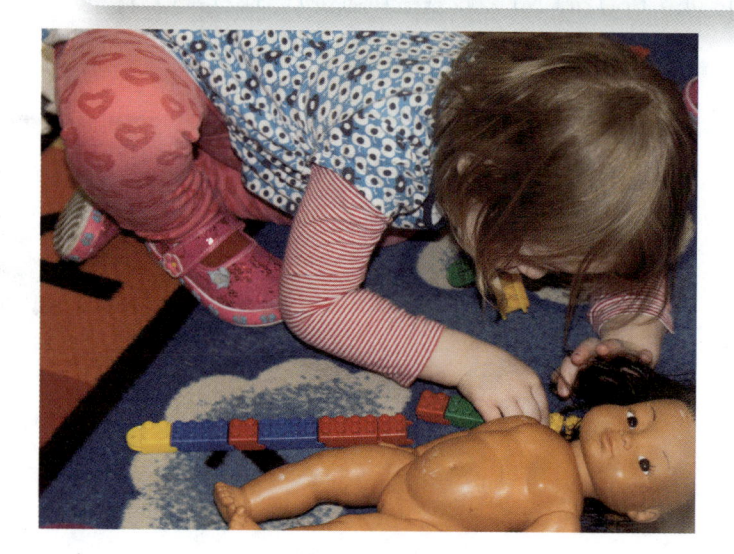

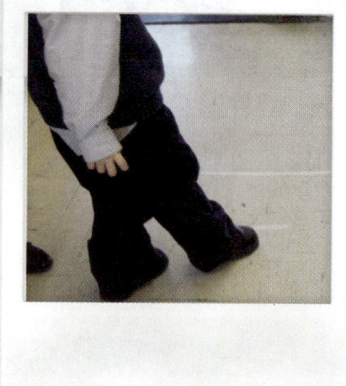

Perimeter

Materials

Rectangular or square shapes such as blocks, books, or boxes

Unit blocks, small glass beads, craft sticks, or other equal-length items

What to Do

Invite children to pick objects to measure and equal-length items to measure with.

Encourage the children to place the measurement items around the perimeter of the object, then lift the measured object out.

The children then count the number of measurement items used.

Circumference

Materials

String

Chenille stems

What to Do

Provide lengths of string or chenille stems for the children to use to measure the circumference of objects. Note: String will retain its shape if dipped into a solution of four parts water and one part glue. Let dry.

Diameter

Materials

String

Scissors

Paper

Glue

Circular objects, such as tops of buckets or containers, blocks

What to Do

Invite children to choose circular objects to measure. Encourage them to measure the distance across with string and cut the string to the length of the distance.

Invite the children to measure the diameters of other objects.

The children can glue the strings to paper to compare the lengths of the diameters.

Label the object measured next to each string. Or children can draw pictures of the objects measured.

Area

Materials

String

Chenille stems

Glass pebbles

What to Do

Provide lengths of string or chenille stems or other materials, such as glass pebbles, for the children to use to measure the area of spaces and shapes. Note: String will retain its shape if dipped into a solution of four parts water and one part glue. Let dry.

Weight

Materials

Scales

Containers of different sizes

What to Do

If they are not already familiar with scales, show the children how to use them. Encourage them to weigh items they find around the room. Model using comparative language, such as *heavy*, *heavier*, *heaviest*, *light*, *lighter*, *lightest*, and so on.

Volume

Materials

Measuring cups

Scoops

Measuring spoons

Containers of different shapes but equal volume

Funnels

Water

Sand

Seeds

Small pebbles

Chapter 7: Measurement

What to Do

Provide containers that are different in shape but hold the same volume. Invite the children to predict which container will hold "more." Then, ask them to test their prediction. Encourage them to explore the concept of volume with different materials and containers.

Seriation

Materials

Nesting cups

Nesting boxes

Dolls in graduated sizes

Blocks in graduated sizes

Pictures in graduated sizes

What to Do

Provide the materials and invite the children to explore ways to arrange them. Model using comparative language such as *big*, *bigger*, *biggest*, *small*, *smaller*, *smallest*, and so on.

Activities for Measuring across the Curriculum

Each center offers opportunities for children to incorporate measuring into their explorations and play.

Art

Weaving

Materials

Weaving frame	Paper strips
Ribbons	Felt strips
Strips of material	Scissors
Chenille stems	Tape

What to Do

A weaving frame can be a mat from a picture frame or a cardboard frame. Provide the materials and invite the children to explore weaving the strips using the words *over*, *under*, *between*, and *through*. Show them how to attach the strips to the frame with tape.

Learning in Action

Amelia described, "This is how I made my weaving picture. First, I measured each ribbon and cut it so it fits the frame. Then I taped it down on the back. Then I made a yellow and pink pattern. Then I measured the purple and sparkly blue ribbons to fit across the other way. I had to go under and over. It took two days to make."

Library Center
Books about Measurement

Materials

Books about measuring, such as:

Davis, Aubrey. 1999. *The Enormous Potato*. Toronto, ON: Kids Can Press.

Fukuda, Toyofumi, and Teruyuki Komida. 2009. *Life-Size Zoo*. New York: Seven Footer Press.

Lionni, Leo. 1960/1988. *Inch by Inch*. New York: Dragonfly.

Murphy, Stuart, and Holly Keller. 1996. *The Best Bug Parade*. New York: HarperCollins.

Tolstoy, Aleksei, and Niamh Sharkey. 2005. *The Gigantic Turnip*. Cambridge, MA: Barefoot Books.

Tompert, Ann. 1996. *Just a Little Bit*. Boston, MA: HMH Books for Young Readers.

What to Do

Read a book that discusses measurement to the children. See what develops!

> Arlene read the story *Life-Size Zoo* by Toyofumi Fukuda and Teruyuki Komida to the children. They became so excited that they decided to create their own pictures of some of the different-sized animals in the book.

Block Center
Measuring Structures
Materials
Blocks
String or yarn
Measuring tape
Yardstick
Unit blocks

What to Do
When the children build structures in the block center, encourage them to measure their creations. They may wish to use nonstandard tools, such as unit blocks, string, or their own hands, or they may choose to use a measuring tape, yardstick, or other standard measuring tool.

Model comparative language such as *tall, taller, tallest, short, shorter, shortest, high, higher, highest,* and so on.

Learning in Action
Mason said, "I am measuring how high my building is."

Carpentry
Measure Twice, Cut Once
Materials

Wood	Saws	Yardstick
Nails	Golf tees	Unit blocks
Screws	Firm foam	Scale
Screwdrivers	String or yarn	
Hammers	Measuring tape	

What to Do

Measuring is a natural activity in the carpentry area. Encourage the children to use nonstandard and standard measurement tools as they build their creations.

Model comparative language.

Learning in Action

Benjamin declared, "My dad said all you have to do is look at the little numbers and you can tell how long it is."

Manipulatives

Measure and Compare

Materials

Beads	Legos
Pegs	String or yarn
Blocks	Scale
Unit cubes	

What to Do

Many opportunities exist—especially for comparisons in height, length, or quantity—in the manipulatives center. As the children explore the materials, encourage them to measure strings of beads, pegs, lined-up toys, interconnecting toys, unit cubes, small blocks, and so on.

Learning in Action

Gavin said, "I am making them all the same."

Outdoor Play

Jump! Jump!

Materials

Measuring tape

String

Rope

What to Do

As the children play outside, encourage them to measure how far each child can jump.

Encourage them to measure the height of a level they jump from.

Encourage them to measure how high they can jump from a standing position.

Create a record over time of how far or high children can jump. Reflect on the data and compare with the children. How much have they grown and changed in their abilities?

Science

Creating Mixtures

Materials

Water

Sand

Salt

Containers

Measuring spoons

Measuring cups

Food coloring

What to Do

Invite the children to create mixtures. For example, how much water is needed to make sand moist enough to mold? How much salt can you add to water until it does not dissolve anymore?

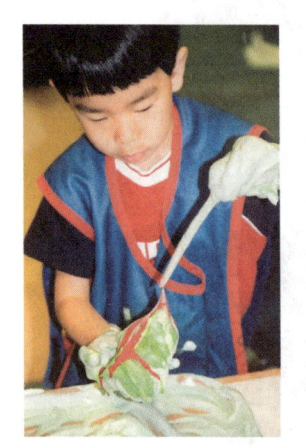

How much dry or wet ingredients do you need to make a mixture more or less sticky?

How much color should you add to make water or sand turn a certain shade?

Measuring Distance

Materials

Toy vehicles

Balls

Ramps

Measuring tape

String or yarn

What to Do

Invite the children to measure the distance a toy vehicle or ball will travel when it is rolled down a ramp. Note: The children can create ramps from planks propped on blocks or can use a marble run.

Encourage them to create two or more ramps and see how far items will travel when rolled.

Making Playdough

Materials

Flour
Salt
Water
Mixing bowls
Spoons
Food coloring or unsweetened drink mix
1-cup measuring cups
½-cup measuring cups
Scoops
Card stock
Photos of the steps to make playdough
Glue

What to Do

Set out the materials in stations along a long table or two tables lined up.

Create picture cards to show the children what to do at each station by gluing a photo of each step onto card stock. Place the cards at the appropriate stations.

Invite the children to begin at station 1 and follow the directions on the card, then proceed to the next station.

- **Station 1 (mixing bowl):** Pick up a bowl to mix in.
- **Station 2 (1-cup measuring cup, scoop, flour):** Measure four 1-cup measures of flour. Children will not need to read the number 4 to understand that four cups are needed. Pour the flour into the bowl.
- **Station 3 (1-cup measuring cup, scoop, salt):** Measure one 1-cup measure of salt. Pour the salt into the bowl with the flour.
- **Station 4 (1-cup and ½-cup measuring cups, water):** Measure one 1-cup measure and one ½-cup measure of water. Pour the water into the bowl with the other ingredients.
- **Station 5 (spoon, food coloring or drink mix):** Mix the ingredients. Add food coloring or unsweetened drink mix to the mixture, if desired.

The children will learn that, to get the consistency they want, they will need to add more water or more flour to the mixture. As they work, model language such as "too sticky" or "too dry."

Playdough will last in the fridge in an airtight container for several days. If it's too dry when brought out, the children can add more water.

Chapter Summary

When children measure, they gain many additional skills:

- Working together to accomplish a task
- Listening to and respecting different perspectives
- Transferring information from one skill to another, such as measuring height with cubes, then measuring length, perimeter, and area using cubes
- Identifying what they have learned
- Representing their learning in their own unique ways

Apply the Learning

1. Identify the resources you have that you can use to engage children in premeasurement activities. What additional resources might you need? Consider the following:
   - Volume
   - Height and length
   - Area
   - Perimeter
   - Weight

2. What skills do you need to consider before you can begin measurement activities with children? Why?

3. What displays might you set up to encourage reflective activities and sustain interest?

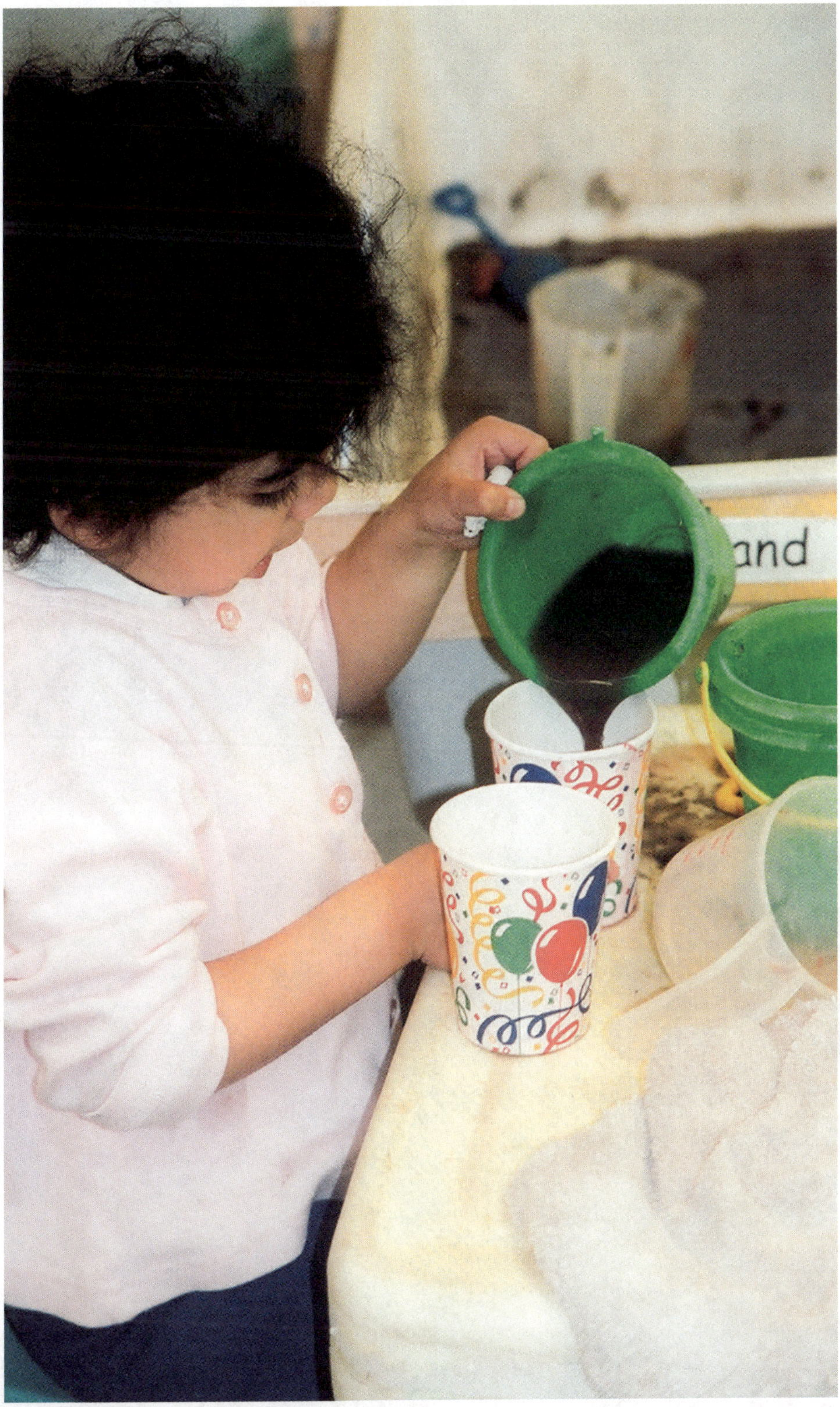
and

CHAPTER 08

Two-and-Three-Dimensional Geometric Shapes

"Investigating and exploring shape and space is an inherent part of children's mathematical development. If you observe the young child playing freely in an outdoor environment, their ability to navigate obstacles, lift, move, or stack objects, or push and pull items are all examples of geometry that come naturally to them."

—Juliet Robertson, *Messy Maths: A Playful Outdoor Approach*

Geometric Shapes Defined

In defining geometric shapes, we consider reasoning about the shape, thinking about how the shapes relate to one another, and thinking about how shapes are perceived in space.

Reasoning about geometric shapes means looking at the physical attributes of different shapes:

- The number of vertices or points, such as three points in a triangle
- Straight or curved lines, such as those in rectangles or ovals
- The number of sides a shape has, such as eight sides to an octagon
- Whether the shapes are flat or curved (2-D or 3-D), such as a circle or a sphere

The second component, thinking about how shapes relate to each other, involves looking at them and seeing how they fit together. For example, two identical squares when placed together form a rectangle, and two identical isolate triangles (triangles with two equal sides) form a rhombus when placed together.

It's also important to look at how shapes are perceived in space. This requires children to learn some of the spatial terminology that supports these perceptions. For example, a ball may be *on* a chair, but the chair is *under* the ball.

Ages and Stages of Understanding Geometric Shapes

Table 8.1: Ages and Stages of Understanding Geometric Shapes

AGES	SKILLS AND ABILITIES
Two to three years old	Matches and sorts shapes that are the same sizes and orientation
Three to four years old	• Recognizes and names common shapes, such as circles, squares, rectangles, and shapes that look like rectangles • Matches shapes of different sizes and orientations
Four to five years old	• Recognizes shapes in different orientations • Constructs known shapes with concrete materials
Five to six years old	• Identifies the components of shapes, such as the number of sides and number of angles • Names rhombus, parallelogram, trapezoid, hexagon, pentagon, octagon, and oval • Differentiates between 2-D and 3-D shapes • Names cones, spheres, cylinders, and cubes

(Crowther, 2018c; Clements and Sarama, 2009, 2019)

The Facilitator's Role

It's important for the facilitator to observe the children in order to provide new shapes and challenges when children are ready, such as a challenge card or a new memory game. Add different materials to the math shelf to expand and maintain the children's interest. Provide opportunities for the children to transfer information they've gained about shapes. For example, take a field trip to identify shapes in buildings, or work with different shapes in a science center.

As the children work with shapes, use vocabulary to describe the shapes and their characteristics.

Model and encourage children to use shape names during math activities. For example, set up visual displays. Take photographs of the children's activities and post these, or use the photos to create shape books for the children to revisit and reflect on past activities. Use teachable moments to label shapes or the components of shapes. Encourage families to participate in shape activities at home.

As with any activity, the facilitator's enthusiasm is one of the keys to engaging in productive activities. Express enthusiasm through your comments, body language, eye contact, a thumbs-up, or a smile. Display materials, resources, and the children's work attractively in the classroom to encourage their interest in the activities. For example, provide materials that spark the imagination, such as items for the light table. Offer materials and experiences that can be used in new situations. For example, the children in the four-year-old room had collected items that represented different shapes. They collaborated to create a display.

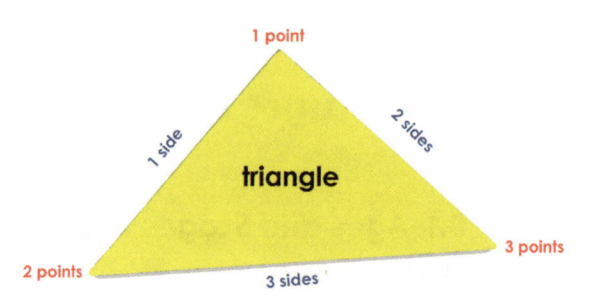

Documenting Understanding Geometric Shapes

For documentation, use tools such as checklists, charts, rubrics, and graphs.

Checklists

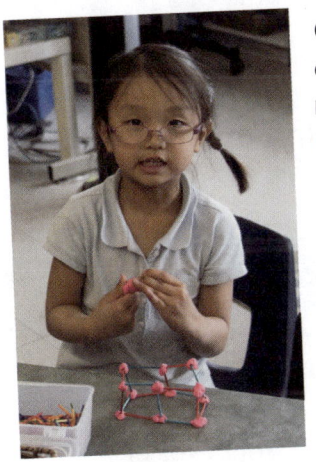

Checklists are easy to use, especially if you observe more than one child on the same tool. Of course, a disadvantage is that a checklist loses much of the richness of other tools, such as dialogue, the descriptions of what the child is doing, or notation of any unusual occurrence. The following are simple checklists to document that children can recognize 2-D and 3-D shapes. When you observe that a child recognizes a specific shape, simply jot the date in the appropriate column. Place tally marks to document that the child has identified the shape at least three times.

Sample 2-D Shapes Checklist

NAME	CIRCLE	RECTANGLE	SQUARE	TRIANGLE	HEXAGON	PENTAGON	OCTAGON
Mei-Ling	5/12/20 II			4/6/20 I			
Susannah	4/10/20 III			4/10/20 II			
Jared	5/13/20 I			4/6/20 III			

Sample 3-D Shapes Checklist

NAME	CUBE	CONE	CYLINDER	PYRAMID	RECTANGULAR PRISM	SPHERE
Jane						
José						
Evie						
Malcolm						

Chapter 8: Two- and Three-Dimensional Geometric Shapes

Charts

A chart will allow you to record more information, including a description of the child's learning and any relevant comments.

Sample Chart for Documenting Understanding of Shapes

Name: Juliette

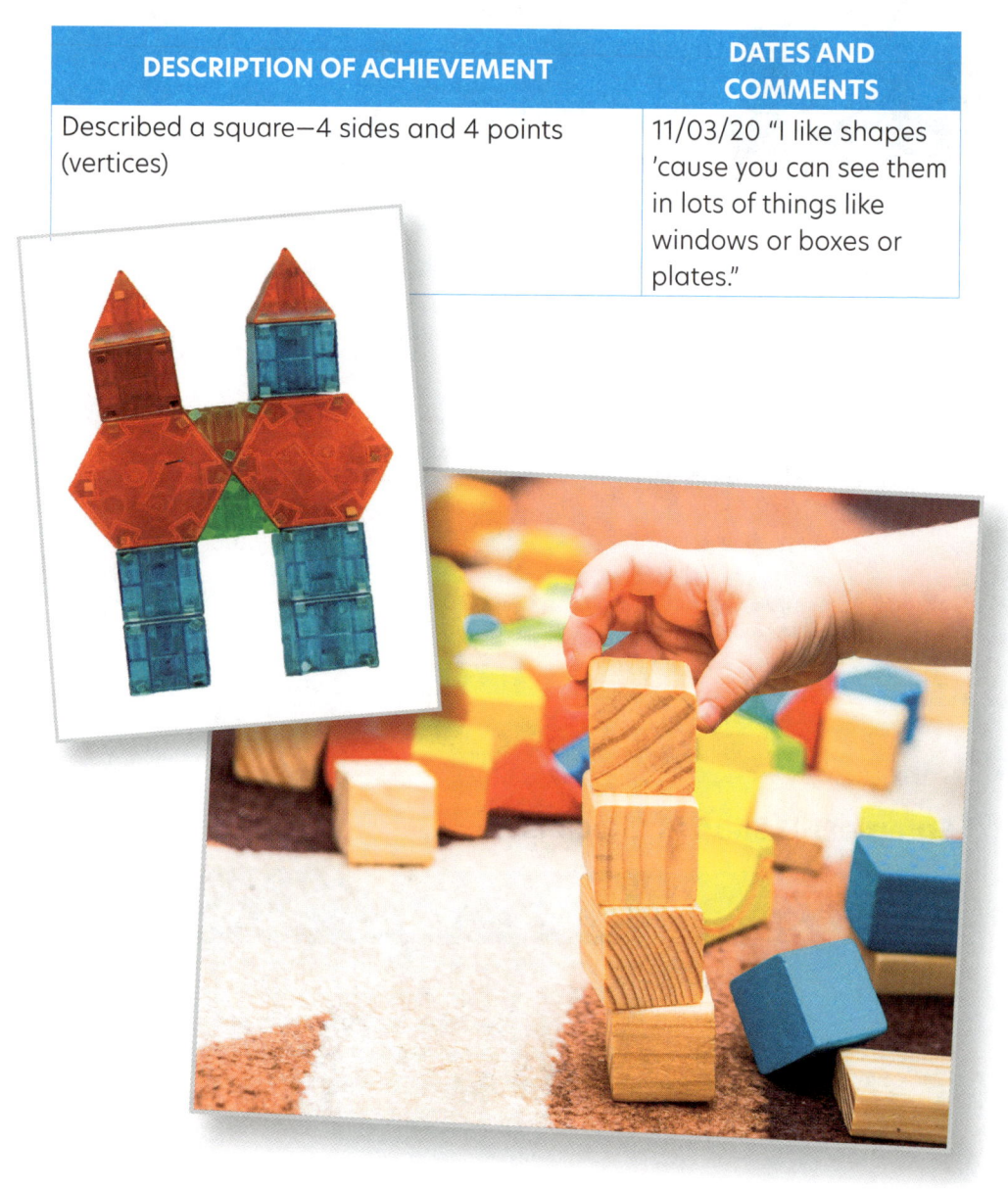

DESCRIPTION OF ACHIEVEMENT	DATES AND COMMENTS
Described a square—4 sides and 4 points (vertices)	11/03/20 "I like shapes 'cause you can see them in lots of things like windows or boxes or plates."

Rubrics

Sample Rubric for Recognizing Shapes

Name: Kaylee

Common shapes include circles, diamonds, hexagons, pentagons, octagons, ovals, parallelograms, rectangles, squares, triangles

Level 1 Matches two identical shapes	**Level 2** Sorts shapes with one difference in shape, size or color	**Level 3** Sorts shapes from more than one difference in shape, size of color	**Level 4** Identifies common shapes by name	**Level 5** Reproduces geometric shapes using various media
			Names all of the above listed shapes consistently 11/16/20	See photo 1, 2, and 3 *
Note: * indicates that validation information is provided on subsequent pages				
Comments:				

Chapter 8: Two- and Three-Dimensional Geometric Shapes

Graphs

Remind the children how to graph their own learning. Create an individual grid for each child, and place one in each math folder.

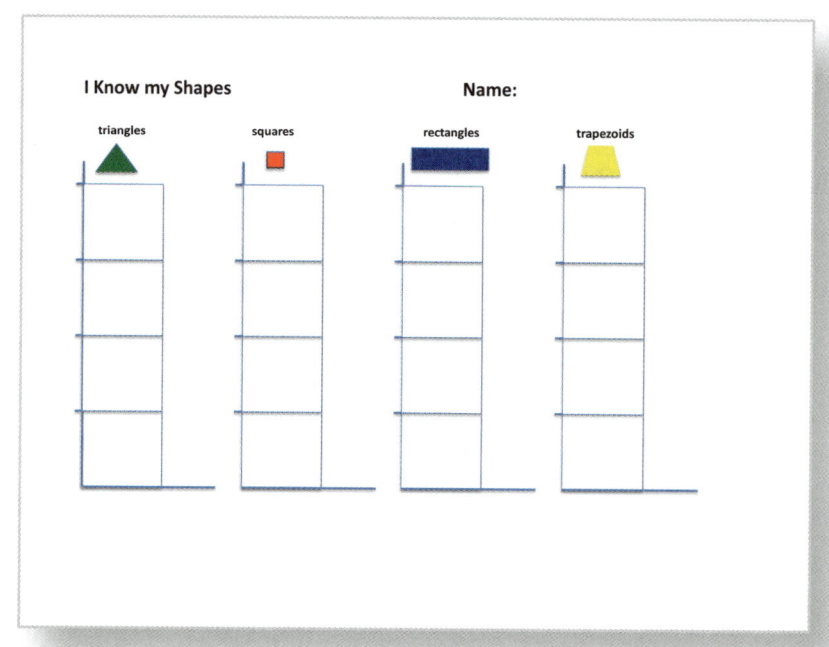

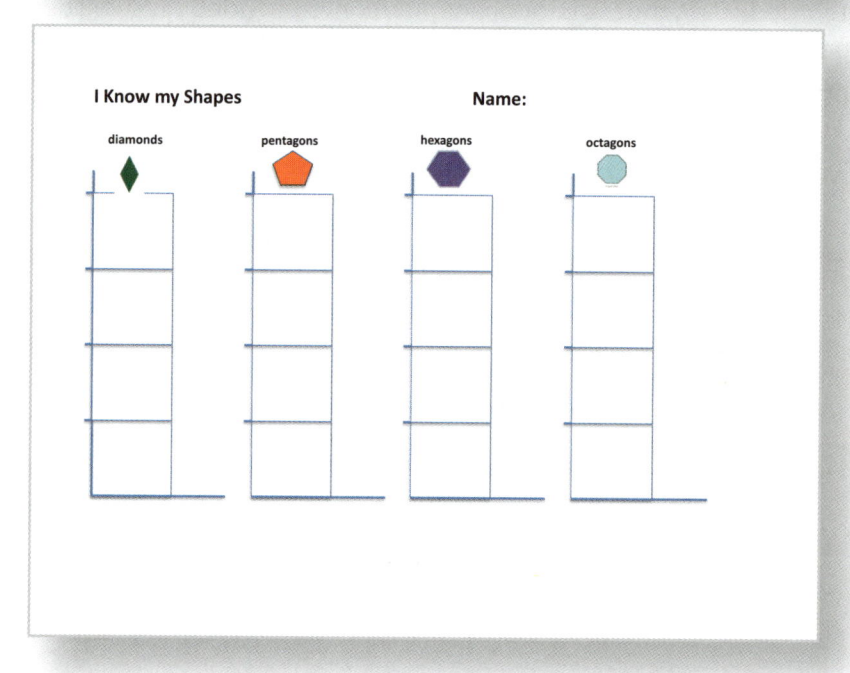

I Know my Shapes Name:

triangles   squares   rectangles   trapezoids

I Know my Shapes Name:

diamonds   pentagons   hexagons   octagons

The Path to Early Math

I Know my Shapes Name:

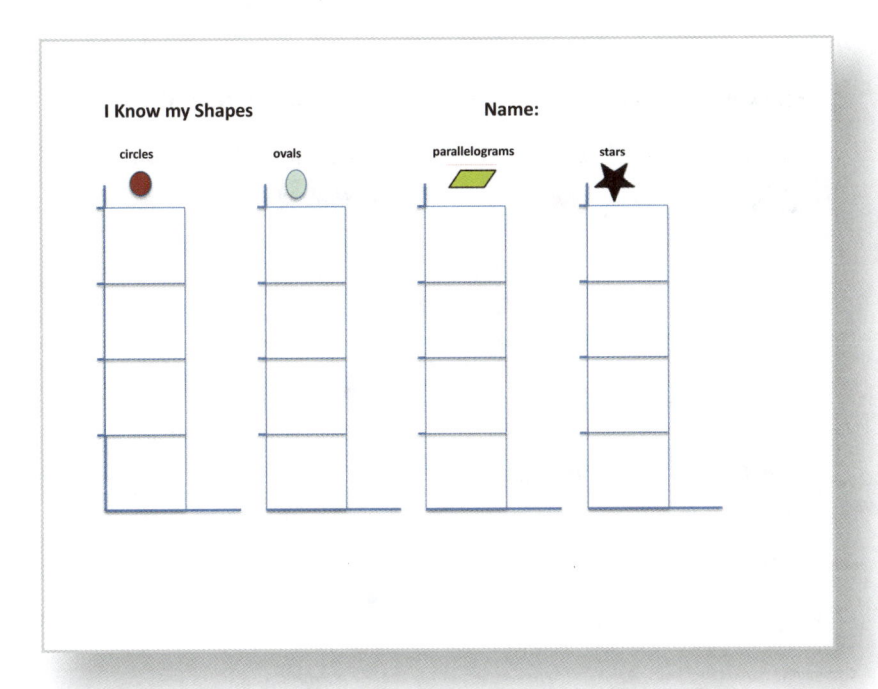

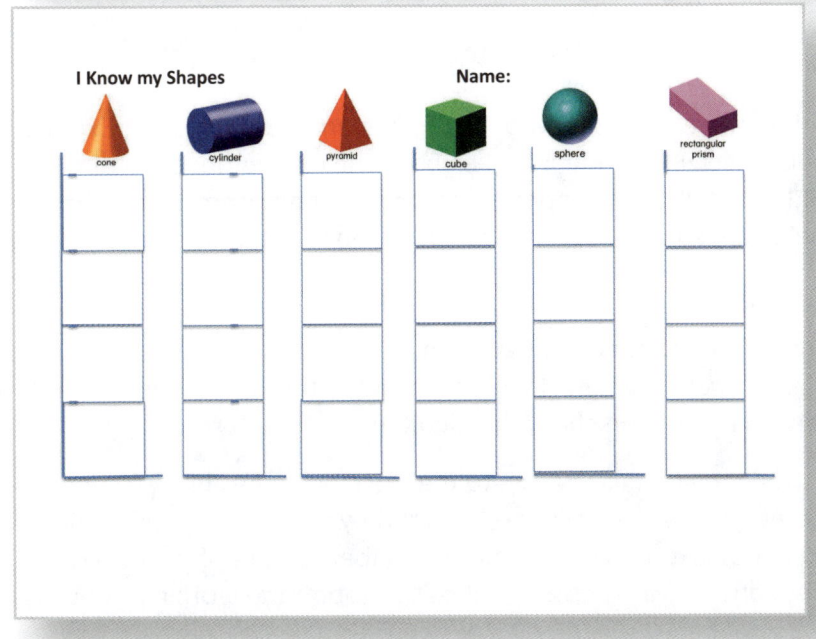

circles   ovals   parallelograms   stars

I Know my Shapes Name:

cone   cylinder   pyramid   cube   sphere   rectangular prism

Chapter 8: Two- and Three-Dimensional Geometric Shapes

I Know my Shapes   **Name: Naomi**

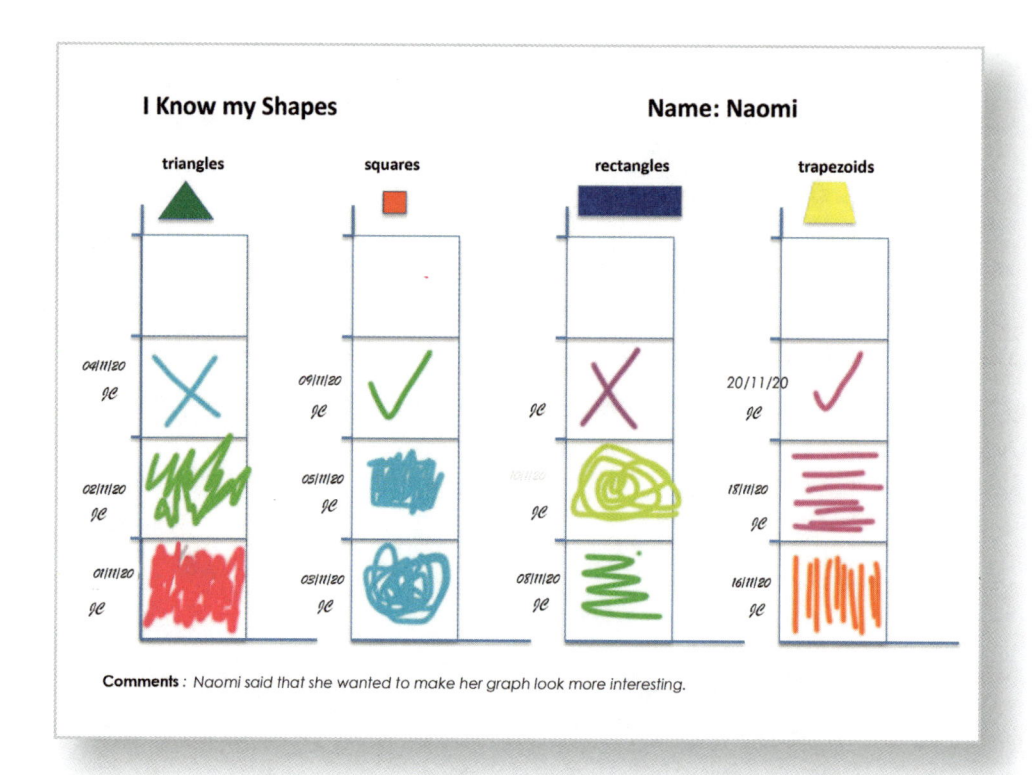

| triangles | squares | rectangles | trapezoids |

Comments: *Naomi said that she wanted to make her graph look more interesting.*

With the children, discuss what a graph is and how it is used. Explain that when a child has identified a shape, he can go get his graph out of his folder and fill in the appropriate squares. Demonstrate how to fill in a graph. For example, if a child has recognized a triangle three times in different situations, he would color in or put an X in three squares (starting at the bottom in the left-hand column). Then, the teacher fills in the date and initials the bottom of the column. When children are ready to proceed on their own, they can tell their teacher when they have identified a shape, and the facilitator can check their learning.

Later, when their families come to the classroom, the children can show them their graphs and talk about what they have learned and what they intend to do next. This makes family members aware of their children's progress and provides opportunities to support the learning at home.

Building Understanding of Geometric Shapes

Children's competency in learning to recognize and learn about shapes depends on their abilities to:

- Compare and match shapes
- Recognize component parts of a shape
- Count accurately to identify aspects of shapes
- Make associations between names and shapes
- Have experiences in manipulating shapes

> **Gavin:** This is a triangle. It has three points and three sides. See? One, two, three points. One, two, three sides.
>
> **Alexander:** I made my building out of squares and triangles. The orange squares made a big rectangle.
>
> **Charlie:** I made a big shape out of triangles. It's sort of a rectangle.

Materials for Understanding Shapes

To give the children a greater awareness of shapes, ask them to help organize the shapes area. Provide containers labeled with the pictures and names of shapes, and encourage the children to organize or reorganize the shape pieces into the containers. As they work, talk with them about what shape they are organizing. Put labels on the open shelves, and help the children put the containers on the right spots on the shelves.

- 2-D Materials
    - » Plastic shapes
    - » Foam shapes
    - » Wooden shapes
    - » Clear shapes
    - » Shapes of different thickness
    - » Magnetic shapes
- 3-D Materials
    - » Plastic shapes
    - » Wooden shapes
    - » Clear shapes
    - » Foam shapes
    - » Magnetic shapes

Talk about how the children could use the shapes in different ways.

In Miss Cara's class, the children identified a number of things they could do with the shapes. They were so excited that they decided to create a book with their suggestions in it.

REGINA: We could make pictures with them.

JAYANTI: We could make new shapes with them.

EUN-JI: We could sort them.

MARIAM: We could stack them.

ANNA: We could put them in order from small to large.

IMANI: I think we could also put them in order from large to small.

GAVIN: We could make patterns. We could trace them. First, I made a size pattern. Then I traced the triangles to make another size pattern.

STUART: We could count them.

ROBERT: We could match them.

The Path to Early Math

Activities to Build Understanding of Geometric Shapes

Numerous activities can build understanding of geometric shapes:

- Matching and sorting
- Building recognition of common shapes
- Constructing shapes
- Identifying components of shapes

Matching and Sorting Shapes

Children's understanding of geometric shapes depends very much on the experiences each child has had. To build strong foundations in this area, children must first be able to recognize geometric shapes. Matching and sorting is an important step. Children can manipulate shapes in a variety of ways to see if they are the same or different.

- Place one shape on top of the other
- Match by placing shapes side by side
- Match by placing the shape on or beside an outline of a shape
- Find matching shapes in the environment

You can help them build these skills through free exploration. Encourage the children to manipulate shapes, organize them in their own way, and use them in whatever fashion they wish. In this way, they will build mental pictures of what shapes look and feel like and how they might be used. In addition, the children will gain an awareness of how objects are used in space, such as on top or beside or in the middle. Sorting shapes into categories, such as all the triangles or all the circles, will help the children recognize different shapes. Once they can match shapes, they can sort the shapes by type, or size, or color.

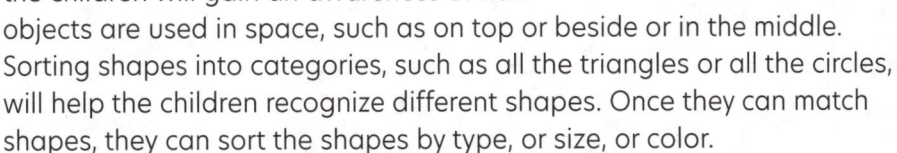

Provide mats that the children can sort the shapes onto, puzzles that require them to find the specific shape and place it into the designated spot, and a variety of materials to explore and build with. For example, children learned how to create their own shape explorations on a scanner. They then printed their presentations. A few days later, on a field trip to the science center, the children discovered that they could rearrange magnetic shapes to roll balls or slide cubes down the wall.

> **Mara:** Look! If the shape is thick, it can stand up. The thin ones can't.
>
> **Dexter:** I sorted my shapes first into mostly purple squares. I then added yellow circles and a green triangle. It turned out to be a building.
>
> **Elijah:** I figured out how to balance things. Usually, you put things on top of each other.

Beyond free exploration, you can provide activities to encourage the children to further develop their skills.

Shapes Challenge Cards

Materials

Printer paper

Construction paper

Scissors

Glue

Pencil

2-D shapes

Clear contact paper or laminator

What to Do

To make a shapes challenge card, cut an 8 ½" x 11" piece of printer paper in half to make a long strip that is 4 ¼" x 11".

Place five or six different shapes on construction paper and trace around them with a pencil.

Cut out the shapes and glue them onto the printer paper. (Be sure to leave some space between each one.)

Place the shapes strip onto a piece of construction paper, and trim around the edges.

Cover the shapes challenge card with clear contact paper or laminate for durability.

Repeat with a different alignment of shapes. Make as many challenge cards as you wish.

Place the mats and the 2-D shapes in the shapes area for the children to explore.

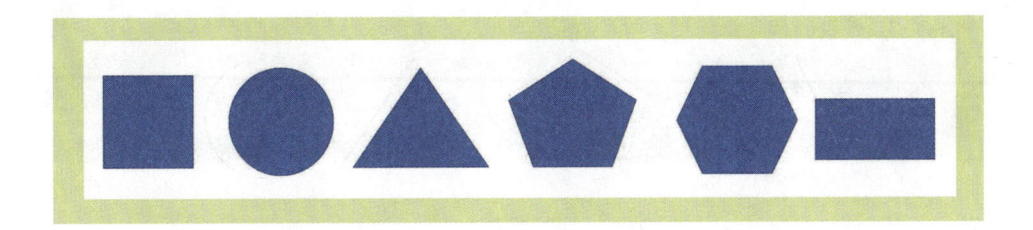

Find-a-Shape Mats

Materials

Construction paper

Label or piece of white paper

Marker

Clear contact paper or laminator

What to Do

On a label or small piece of white paper, draw or place two shapes cut out of colored paper. Write, "Find [shape]s and [shape]s." For example, write, "Find circles and triangles."

Place the label at the top of a large piece of construction paper.

Cover the find-a-shape mat with clear contact paper or laminate for durability. Make several mats with different shapes.

Place the mats and containers of mixed shapes in the shapes area. Encourage the children to place the shapes on the mat that match the label.

For children who need a little help, ask them to find all of one shape. For example, "Find all of the squares and put them on the mat."

Memory Games

Materials

Card stock or index cards

Markers

Ruler

What to Do

Create a set of playing cards with shapes on them, making two of each card. Be sure to draw the shapes carefully and make each pair of cards match exactly. Create cards for circles, squares, rectangles, rhombuses, triangles, hexagons, pentagons, and octagons.

Shuffle the cards, turn them facedown, and spread them out over a table. Invite the children to take turns picking one card and then drawing another card to try to find the match. If the child makes a match, he keeps the matching set. If he doesn't make a match, he returns the cards to the pile and waits until his next turn to try again.

Shapes Search

Materials

2-D shapes

Construction paper

Scissors

Painter's tape

Basket

What to Do

Make exact outlines of shapes on construction paper, and cut them out.

Tape the shapes to various surfaces around the room.

Place a selection of 2-D shapes in a basket, and encourage the children to pick one out and then match it to a shape posted in the room. Name the shapes the children are looking for. This activity also works very well outside.

Building Recognition of Common Shapes

As children gain experiences with matching and sorting shapes, model using the names of the shapes: "Catherine, I see you're making something with triangles and rectangles. Tell me about what you're making." Go for a walk around the neighborhood and play I Spy as you look for shapes. Play guessing games: "I have a shape behind my back that has four equal sides and four points. What is it?" Read books about shapes.

Books about Shapes

Berenstain, Stan, and Jan Berenstain. 1968. *The Berenstain Bears Inside, Outside, Upside Down.* New York: Random House.

Dodds, Dayle Ann. 1996. *The Shape of Things.* Somerville, MA: Candlewick.

Hutchins, Pat. 1987. *Changes, Changes.* New York: Simon and Schuster.

Light, Steven. 2015. *Have You Seen My Monster?* Somerville, MA: Candlewick.

Maranke, Rinck, and Martijn van der Linden. 2017. *Tangram Cat.* London, UK: Lemniscaat.

May, Eleanor. 2013. *Mice on Ice.* New York: Kane Press.

Micklethwait, Lucy. 2004. *I Spy Shapes in Art.* New York: HarperCollins.

Murphy, Stuart J. 1998. *Circus Shapes.* New York: HarperCollins.

Pluckrose, Henry. 2018. *Shapes.* New York: Scholastic.

Walsh, Ellen Stoll. 2007. *Mouse Shapes.* New York: Houghton Mifflin Harcourt.

Shapes Path

Materials

Construction paper

Scissors

Clear contact paper or laminator

Painter's tape

What to Do

Create a path of 2-D shapes to walk on at the entrance to the room. You can do this by simply placing painter's tape on the floor in different geometric shapes, or you can cut large geometric shapes out of construction paper, laminate or cover them with clear contact paper, and tape them to the floor.

Encourage the children to step on, jump on, or walk around a shape that you call out. You could also play this game outside, drawing shapes with sidewalk chalk. Encourage families to participate in this activity when they drop off their children.

Shape Cube

Materials

Square cardboard box

Construction paper

Clear contact paper

Scissors

Container of 2-D shapes

What to Do

Create a die out of a cardboard box. If you have a cube-shaped box, use that. If not, cut six 5-inch squares out of cardboard, and tape them together in a cube shape with painter's tape.

Cut out six shapes from construction paper, choosing from among a circle, square, rectangle, triangle, rhombus, pentagon, hexagon, oval, and octagon. Adhere one shape per side to the cube using clear contact paper.

Provide a container of the 2-D shapes that are represented on the cube.

Invite the children to roll the shape cube, find the shape that's on the top, identify it, and then find that shape in the shapes container.

Give each child a turn, repeating the process.

Shapes Twist

Materials

Clear plastic shower curtain

Acrylic paint

Paintbrushes

Painter's tape

What to Do

On one side of a shower curtain, paint shapes using acrylic paint: circle, square, rectangle, triangle, oval, rhombus, pentagon, hexagon, and octagon. Let dry.

Lay the painted shower curtain on the floor, painted side down, and secure it in place with painter's tape.

Invite the children to play a game in which each child puts a body part on the shape you call out: "Put your hand on the octagon." "Put your foot on the rhombus." "Put your other hand on the circle."

Constructing Shapes

Once the children begin to construct their own shapes, their understanding of shapes will increase dramatically. Add new materials to the shapes area to encourage them to construct shapes.

- Magnetic building tiles: These types of shapes are excellent for constructing different geometric shapes, both 2-D and 3-D.
- Small sticks, toothpicks, and playdough or mini marshmallows

The Path to Early Math

- String, chenille stems, playdough, scissors, glue, and construction paper
- Tracing forms, plastic shapes, markers, paper, pencils, or colored pencils: Ask the children to identify the shapes they make. Write the shape name under the shape, if the child wants you to.
- Sponge printmaking shapes, paint, paper, plastic plates
- Paper straws and connectors
- Craft sticks and playdough or glue

Outdoors, provide chalk and a chalkboard or let the children use the chalk on the pavement. They also can draw shapes with sticks or their fingers in the dirt.

Identifying Components of Shapes

This is perhaps the most difficult step in the identification of shapes. When children have had many experiences exploring, using, creating with, and identifying shapes, as well as hearing the names of the shapes, identifying the components of shapes becomes much easier. You can use a number of strategies to help children develop skills at recognizing the components of shapes: vertices or points, and sides or faces. For example, create a display that identifies the number of points and sides or faces of a variety of shapes. Create a set of shapes with labels to identify the characteristics of each shape.

Table 8.2: 2-D Shape Components

SHAPE		COMPONENTS
Circle	●	A round shape with no corners or edges
Oval	●	A curved shape with no corners or edges that resembles the outline of an egg
Triangle	▲	• 3 points (vertices) and 3 sides • Sides can be equal or unequal
Square	■	• 4 points (vertices) and 4 sides • All sides are equal
Rectangle	▬	• 4 points (vertices) and 4 sides • Horizontal sides are equal • Vertical sides are equal
Parallelogram	▰	• 4 points (vertices) and 4 sides • The opposite sides are equal
Pentagon	⬠	• 5 points (vertices) • 5 equal sides
Hexagon	⬢	• 6 points (vertices) • 6 equal sides
Octagon	⬣	• 8 points (vertices) • 8 equal sides

Table 8.3: 3-D Shape Components

SHAPE		COMPONENTS
Pyramid		• 5 points (vertices) • 5 triangular faces • 8 sides
Cone		• 1 point called an apex or vertex • 1 circular base
Rectangular prism		• 8 points (vertices) • 6 faces • Each face is a rectangle

Cube	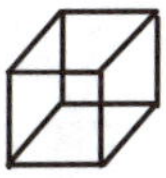	• 8 points (vertices) • 6 faces • Each face is a square
Cylinder	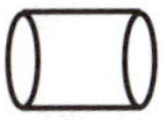	• 2 equal flat ends that are circles or ovals • Continuous curve around sides
Triangular prism		• 6 points (vertices) • 5 faces
Sphere		• a round solid shape that looks like a ball

Counting Shape Characteristics

Materials

Basket or other container

2-D shapes: circle, square, rectangle, triangle, hexagon, octagon, oval, rhombus

3-D shapes: sphere, pyramid, cube, cylinder, rectangular prism, cone, triangular prism, pentangular prism

What to Do

Invite each child to pick a shape out of a basket and count the number of sides, faces, or points it has. Engage them in identifying the components as they look at the shapes.

Encourage them to identify the shapes. (Help as needed.)

Shapes Challenge Cards

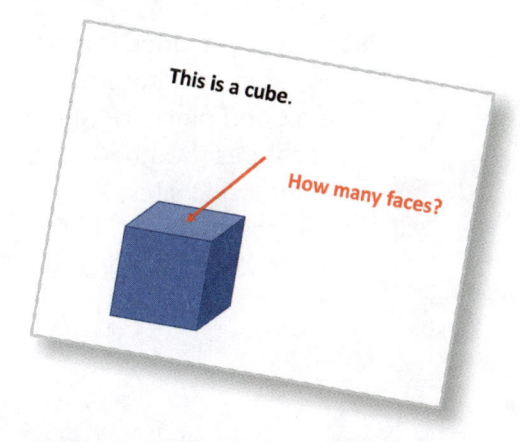

Materials

Card stock

Images of 2-D and 3-D shapes

Marker

Glue

What to Do

Create challenge cards for each of the shapes. On a piece of card stock, glue an image of a shape. Using a marker, write the name of the shape on the card, and draw an arrow to a component of the shape, a face or point. Write a question, such as "How many faces does it have?" "How many points does it have?"

Create a challenge for the day and post it in the shapes area. Read the challenge card for the day to the children. They can respond by finding the materials that they'd like to use to create the shape. For example, Edward created his challenge of a cylinder using bendable wires.

Children may also create their own challenge cards to post.

Chapter Summary

As children explore shapes, they also learn to identify shapes that are seen from different perspectives. Shapes look different in different alignments or at different distances. Awareness and understanding of shapes lead to building strong foundations for academic skills through the school years, as well as to becoming aware of and recognizing different perspectives.

Apply the Learning

1. Shape exploration is exciting for children, especially when they can see shapes in their natural environments. Identify areas nearby that would be a good place for the children to look for and identify shapes. Note the shapes that they could find there, and then plan a field trip. Consider the following sites:
   - Neighborhoods
   - Your school building
   - Parks

- Museum
- Science center
- Playgrounds

2. Prepare free-choice activities to invite children to create shape pictures or structures.
   - Post photographs of buildings familiar to the children, and encourage them to build a structure out of blocks.
   - Provide paint and sponges of different shapes, and encourage the children to create structures both real and imaginary. In the art area, post photos of structures or buildings painted by artists.
   - Create a display of famous 3-D buildings such as the Great Pyramids of Giza, octagonal houses, or the Pentagon in Washington, DC. Provide 3-D shapes so that children can compare and match the shapes to the buildings posted.

3. How might you encourage families to participate in their children's learning about shapes? Consider the following:
   - Newsletters
   - Postings informing families of current topics
   - Encouraging families to help collect pictures and photographs of interesting shape structures
   - Inviting families to do presentations or demonstrations to children

CHAPTER 09

Parts and Wholes:
Beginning Understanding of Fractions

"It is important that students meet various representations of fractions early on, with different meanings and different types of wholes representations. It is also important that they practice partitioning wholes of various types."

—Marian Small, *Making Math Meaningful for Canadian Students K-8*

Parts and Wholes Defined

In the simplest terms, parts and wholes can be described as breaking down a set of objects into equal parts. When children have had experiences in working with geometric shapes, this task becomes much easier. Geometric shapes are ideal to encourage the understanding of parts and wholes. For example, two squares when placed together make a rectangle; therefore, we have two equal parts.

Children learn about parts and wholes very early. They learn it when they share things equally, such as cutting a pie into six equal pieces (one for each family member), slicing fruit into equal pieces to share, splitting a group of toys equally to share with each other, and talking about terms associated with parts and wholes, such as *all gone*, *empty*, *full*, *half full*, and *half empty*.

Ages and Stages of Understanding Parts and Wholes

Much of children's understanding is based on previous experiences with geometric shapes and incidental learning, such as sharing half a cookie or dividing a pie into six equal parts.

Table 9.1: Ages and Stages of Understanding Parts and Wholes

AGES	SKILLS AND ABILITIES
Three years old	• Combines two shapes to form a whole • Splits a whole into two equal parts
Three to four years old	Combines more than two shapes to form a whole or splits a whole into equal parts
Four to five years old	Verbalizes how many parts are in a whole: "This square has four equal triangles."
Five to six years old	Creates structures or designs using parts and wholes and various types of media. "I made buildings. I used seven and three and five and five orange squares to make rectangles for skyscrapers."

(Crowther, 2018c)

The Facilitator's Role

One of the key roles for the facilitator is to develop the appropriate language skills to increase the understanding of parts and wholes, such as *full, empty, half, quarter, third, half full, half empty,* and *one and a half*. Provide models and demonstrations of what numerical fractions look like: ½, ⅓, ¼. Observe children to identify teachable moments where you can reinforce language skills.

Spend time creating opportunities and activities to demonstrate and explore composing and decomposing shapes and objects into parts and wholes. As you observe the children engaging in the activities, notice which materials need to be changed, adapted, or added to maintain their interest. Encourage collaboration activities with family and community members to provide opportunities to share materials and resources to enhance understanding of parts and wholes.

Create documentation panels to encourage children to reflect on past experiences and build new ones. For example, make a parts-and-wholes display:

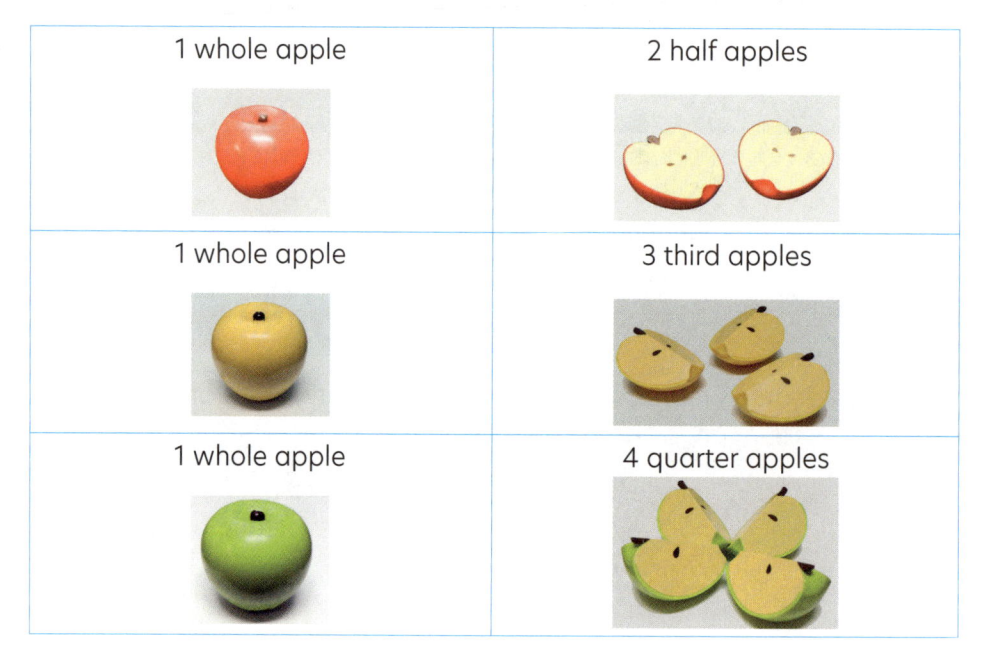

1 whole apple	2 half apples
1 whole apple	3 third apples
1 whole apple	4 quarter apples

Documenting Understanding Parts and Wholes

You can easily document children's explorations and understanding through booklets and rubrics.

Parts and Wholes Booklets

As the children engage in activities, create booklets that contain a combination of diagrams, photographs, and written descriptions dictated by them as an ongoing demonstration of skills and concepts. Booklets clearly show what the child has learned and her progress, as well as her individuality, creativity, and thinking. A booklet is easy to include in any other documentation package, such as a rubric or a portfolio, and is an easy methodology to share with family members. Store the booklets in an accessible location, and encourage the children to share their booklets with their families at pick-up times.

"I made two rectangles with playdough and craft sticks and put them together. I have two halves. One half on one side and one on the other."

"I like drawing. I drew a triangle and a square and now I am drawing a rectangle. The triangle has two parts, so it has two halves. The square has four parts. Each one is a quarter."

Rubrics

As discussed in previous chapters, a rubric is an excellent documentation strategy that can be adapted to any format: comments only or a combination of comments, photographs, and other artifacts. The information from the children's booklets can be included in their folders with the rubrics. Consider keeping the folders in a confidential and secure area, filed under the children's names, and sharing this information with family members at pick-up times.

Sample Parts and Wholes Rubric

Name: Nash

Level 1	Level 2	Level 3	Level 4
Combines two shapes to form a whole, such as two half circles make a whole circle	Combines more than two shapes to form a whole, such as four wedges make a circle	Verbalizes parts of a whole, such as, "Two triangles make a square."	Creates structures or designs using parts and wholes and various media
	5/17/20: Combined 3 squares to form a rectangle 5/26/20: Combined 4 triangles to make a square 6/7/20: Combined 3 triangles to form a trapezoid	5/17/20: "I put three squares together, and I made a rectangle." 5/26/20: "I made a square out of four triangles." 6/7/20: "I put three triangles together. I made a trapezoid."	6/7/20: Created a mirror image with tangrams 6/17/20: Made a picture with Carlos and Kaya and said it was a "liserbird." 6/17/20: Helped create a diagram; each child added a shape of choice, then identified that shape

Comments:

Building Understanding of Parts and Wholes

When children engage in parts-and-wholes activities, they gain experiences and greater understanding of constructing a variety of shapes with a different number of equal parts, constructing and deconstructing shapes into their component parts, and understanding simple fractions such as one half or one quarter.

Many of the materials mentioned in chapter 8 are useful for understanding parts and wholes; however, the way you use the materials is specific to encouraging a child's understanding of this topic.

In the shapes area, provide triangles, half circles, squares, rectangles, pentagons, and trapezoids, along with the containers for each type of shape. Encourage the children to combine two or more shapes to form a new whole shape. Encourage them to split a whole shape into two or more equal parts.

Add 3-D shapes, such as cubes and rectangular prisms. Encourage the children to form combinations of shapes and talk about how many parts are in the whole.

> Greg said, "I made a huge rectangle. I used fifteen squares to make it."

Add 2-D and 3-D magnetic geometric shapes. The children can create or combine magnetic shapes to form new shapes. Add parts-and-wholes toy sets, such as magnetic pizzas and magnetic apple fractions.

Add fraction shapes, such as circles, triangles, squares, rectangles, ovals, trapezoids, and hexagons. You can create these by drawing the shapes and cutting them into equal slices.

Activities for Parts and Wholes across the Curriculum

As children learn about part and wholes, they gain the understanding that things can be broken into equal parts. That leads to the understanding of the associated vocabulary such as *two halves* or *three thirds*. However, children also need experiences with wholes that can be broken into unequal parts, to gain a solid foundation for understanding fractions later on. Fractions can be broken into equal parts or unequal parts. At this point, it is easier simply to talk about fractions as parts of an object. Use a variety of activities to help the children understand that some items can be broken down into parts and wholes, but the parts may not be equal. This is an important distinction that they need to learn.

Activities for Parts and Wholes Across the Curriculum

Art

Unequal Parts

Materials

Craft sticks	Printmaking materials	Glue
Small sticks	Paper	Pebbles
Paper strips	Playdough	Shells
Paint	Pompoms	Paintbrushes

What to Do

One of the best ways to encourage children to recognize and create unequal sets is to begin the process with a dialogue about what they have observed or are currently engaged in.

After the first snowfall, the children in the preschool room were busily engaged in creating snowmen. One group used white playdough. Another drew snowmen with white chalk on a black paper or drew them on various colors of paper with markers. A third group was painting white snowmen on various colors of paper.

As the children's teacher, Shelagh, observed this, she asked them about their snowmen. "How many parts does your snowman have?" She got various answers from two parts to five parts. She then asked, "Are all the parts the same?" All the children answered that they were different because they were different sizes.

Shelagh then explained, "That's why we have to talk about parts of the snowmen because they are not the same. We can only call the parts of the snowmen *halves* or *thirds* or *fourths* or *fifths* when each part is equal."

Blocks

Building Parts and Wholes

Materials

Blocks in a variety of sizes

What to Do

As the children play and build with the blocks, engage them in talking about the parts and wholes of their creations. For example, ask, "How many parts are in your tower?" "Are all the parts the same?" "How many parts are in the whole castle?"

Learning in Action

> Learning to share is a good way to teach about fractions. Miss Tamiko heard three boys arguing about how many cars each could use.
>
> **SEBASTIEN:** I need a lot 'cause I want to run them down my ramp.
>
> **MALCOLM:** But then there won't be enough for us to race on our track.
>
> **JOSÉ:** How 'bout we count them out. Put them all in a big pile.
>
> The boys decided to share by each choosing one car at a time until each one had five cars. They were satisfied that they each had enough.

Books

Mix and Match

Materials

Variety of flip books

What to Do

Place flip books in the library area for the children to look at. Flip books that ask children to form new things from two or three parts will help them develop the understanding that sometimes parts are not equal. Plus, they're fun!

Books for Understanding Parts and Wholes

Berger, Carin. 2006. *All Mixed Up: A Mix-and-Match Book*. San Francisco, CA: Chronicle Books.

Fox, Woody. 2007. *Animals: A Mix-and-Match Book*. Greensboro, NC: Carson-Dellosa.

Isaacs, Connie, and Barry Green. 2019. *Mix and Match Monsters*. Mineola, NY: Dover Publications.

Laberis, Stephanie. 2012. *Mix and Match Zoo Animals*. Mineola, NY: Dover Publications.

Moriuchi, Mique. 2007. *Mix and Match Animals*. Atlanta, GA: Piggy Toes Press.

Manipulatives

Ways to Make Five

Materials

Unit cubes

Cuisenaire rods

What to Do

Children can use unit cubes to create sets of different numbers. For example, challenge them to create as many sets adding up to five cubes as they can: one cube and four cubes, two cubes and three cubes, zero cubes and five cubes.

When you observe that a child has created a set that adds to five, use language to introduce the concept of fractions.

Learning in Action

Annie had created different sets of five.

Ms. Yan: Great job, Annie. I see this set has one fifth and four fifth.

Annie: And see? This set has three fifth and two fifth.

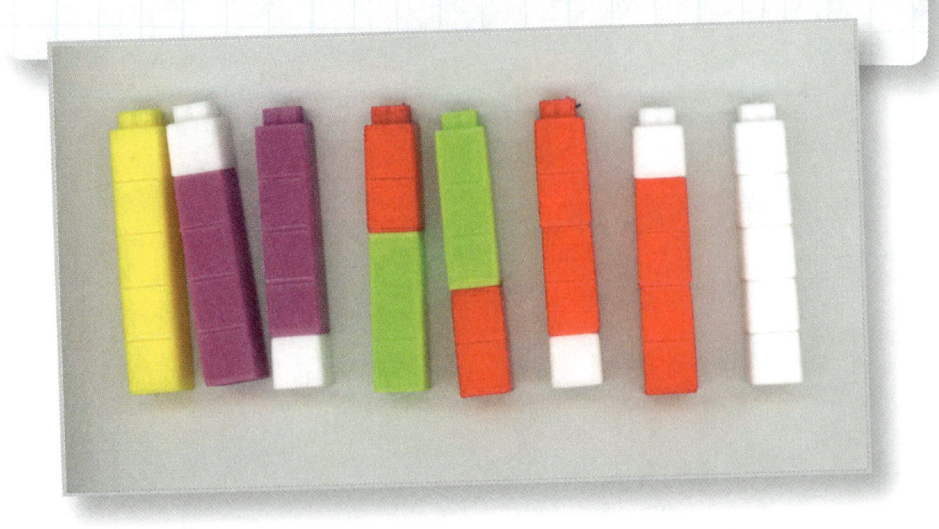

Puzzles and Games

Puzzle Parts and Wholes

Materials

Puzzles

What to Do

Puzzles lend themselves to discussions about unequal parts. As the children engage in putting puzzles together, talk with them about the number of parts.

Learning in Action

When Brennan finished putting the snake puzzle together, he announced, "The snake puzzle has ten parts."

Picture Mix and Match

Materials

Photos of the children

Scissors

Clear contact paper or laminator

What to Do

Children enjoy photos of themselves and their classmates. Take a photo of each child standing and looking directly at the camera, as well as photos of the children's faces.

Print each photo, and cut it exactly in half horizontally. Cover each half with clear contact paper or laminate for durability. Put the pieces in the puzzle area.

The children can then mix and match their faces or bodies. As they work, engage them in talking about parts and wholes.

Nature Fractions

Materials

Natural materials, such as leaves, feathers, rocks, and flowers

Camera

Printer

Card stock

Scissors

Clear contact paper or laminator

What to Do

When children are outside, encourage them to find interesting objects such as feathers, leaves, rocks, or dandelions. When a child finds something, photograph the item.

Inside, print the images. Place each photo on a piece of card stock, and cover it with clear contact paper or laminate it for durability.

Cut each card into equal parts, such as halves, thirds, quarters, or fifths.

Encourage the children to put the parts together and articulate how many equal parts there are and what the associated fraction is.

As the children become more adept at identifying the number of parts and the associated fractions, they could play this as a card game for a small group. To play the game, pile the card pieces in the center. The children take turns collecting one card at a time to try to complete an entire image. They each lay their cards faceup in front of them. When it is their turn, they can either pick up a new card or negotiate a trade with another player. They play until all the matches are made to complete the images.

Learning in Action

Jonathan had three-fourths of a stone. He noticed that Jenny had the other piece.

JONATHAN: I'll trade you one of my cards for your one-fourth of a stone.

JENNY: Okay.

Jenny traded her stone card for the one-fourth feather card that Jonathan had.

Sand and Water Center
Measuring Parts and Wholes
Materials

Water

Sand

Sand and water table or tubs

Measuring cups in a variety of sizes

What to Do

Activities with sand or water (or during cooking experiences) are ideal to help children identify parts and wholes while measuring. Measuring cups are also useful for creating understanding of fractions.

Children can fill and pour using a quarter cup to fill a whole cup. This activity will help them see how many quarter cups of water or sand will fill a whole cup.

Learning in Action

Ben decided to measure how many quarter cups of water it would take to fill a 1-cup container, then to compare that to how many ¼-cups of sand it would take to fill a 1-cup container. He was surprised that water and sand took four ¼-cups each to fill a 1-cup container.

Seriation Cups

Materials

Nesting or stacking cups

What to Do

Seriation cups (also called nesting or stacking cups) are an excellent tool to help children gain an understanding of fractions. With younger children, begin by using fewer pieces.

As children explore the cups, they can learn how many cups can fit into the whole. Help them learn such language as *one third*, *two thirds*, and *three thirds*, as you describe what they are doing.

Learning in Action

Nathaniel had started with four seriation cups. He fit each cup into the next largest cup, then he counted them. He said, "Four cups." Pointing, he identified each one, "This is one fourth. This is two fourth. This is three fourth. And this is four fourth."

Outdoor Play

Equal Sets

Materials

Natural materials, such as leaves, sticks, stones, acorns, pine cones, and shells

What to Do

Invite the children to find natural materials.

Encourage them to create equal sets of the materials found. They could draw squares in the sandbox or on the ground, and then put their sets in the squares—for example, half the pine cones in one square and half in another.

Learning in Action

When children are able to create their own understanding of fractions, it is evident that they understand that concept. For example, Mara created geometric shapes using small colored sticks. She then divided them in half by using one additional stick. She said, "I have two half triangles and two half rectangles."

Snack Time

Cutting Fruit

Materials

Variety of fruit

Plastic knives

Plates, napkins

What to Do

Snack time is a great opportunity for reinforcing understanding of parts, wholes, and fractions. Invite the children to help make snack. Have them wash their hands first.

Let them have easy-to-cut fruit, such as strawberries. Encourage them to use a knife to cut the fruit into pieces, and talk with them as they do.

Learning in Action

Malachai was helping to create his own snack. As he cut up a strawberry, he said, "I'm cutting it into half." When he looked at it and compared the two pieces, he said, "Not quite a half." Pointing to one piece, he commented, "This side is bigger than that one."

Chapter Summary

Children need a firm foundation to construct and deconstruct materials into parts and wholes. Identifying unequal component parts in seriation or puzzle activities, understanding that a whole can be created with many parts but that these parts are not equal, and identifying equal parts, such as the parts of an apple cut into equal pieces or a rectangle split into four equal sections, will give them the foundation to understand parts and wholes. Explorations of parts and wholes in the early years leads to the eventual understanding of fractions.

Apply the Learning

1. What activities and routines during the day lend themselves to discussions about parts and wholes? How would you best organize the necessary materials for the activities? What language concepts can you enhance during these activities?

2. Collect some recipes that children can make for snacks or lunches. What vocabulary could you enhance when the children follow the recipes?

3. Sand and water are natural areas for developing parts and whole activities. List three activities for the sand and water areas that would support understanding of parts and wholes.

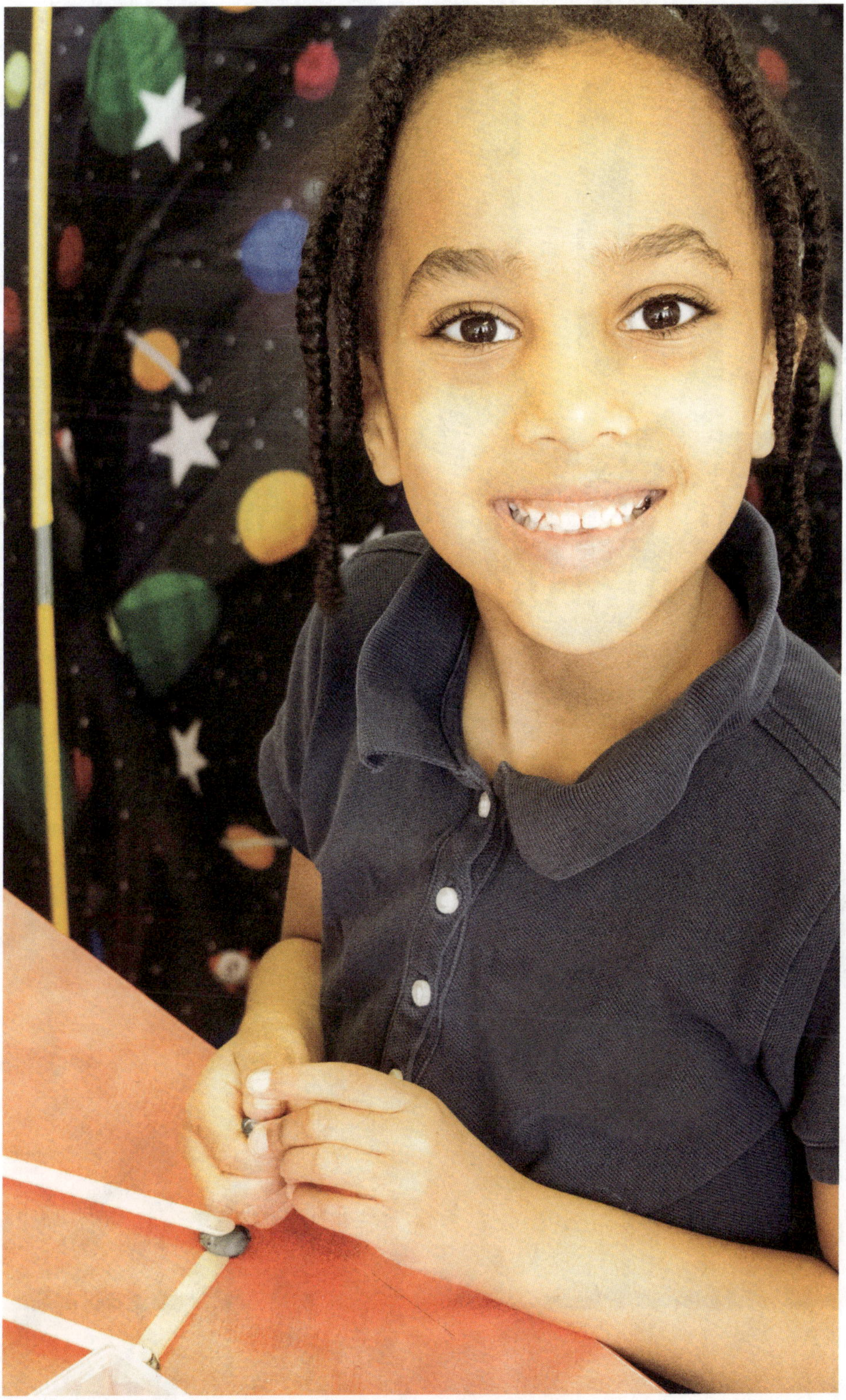

CHAPTER 10

Computation: Addition and Subtraction

"As a child comes to understand more, the child's problem-solving method becomes more integrated internally and in relation to other methods. As a method becomes more automatic, reflection about some aspects may become possible, leading to new understanding."

—Jeremy Kilpatrick, W. Gary Martin, and Deborah Schifter, *A Research Companion to Principles and Standards for School Mathematics*

Addition and Subtraction Defined

The simplest definition of *addition* is to combine two or more numbers or objects and state how many there are in total. Similarly, a simple definition of *subtraction* is taking one or more numbers or items away from another number or set and answering the question of how many are left. Any computational activities with young children should be with concrete materials that they can manipulate.

Simple addition and subtraction occur very early as a child learns to share—two cookies, one for the child and one for a friend. More formal addition and subtraction emerges with the child's abilities to engage in one-to-one correspondence, combine sets, object count, and continue to count from a known number.

Children learn to share items by giving one item to each of the participants (including the child) one at a time, until all children have the same number of items.

> Four boys were engaged in rolling marbles down a marble run. One of the boys was quick to pick up all the marbles, so the other boys complained. Ms. Jennifer approached the boys and commented, "You seem to have a problem sharing the marbles. How could we solve this problem?" The boys thought about it and decided they could share all the marbles and that each boy should have the same number. They divided the marbles using one-to-one correspondence. Two were left over, so they decided not to use these two at all and returned them to the marble container.

Children need experiences combining two or more sets into one set; for example, combining a set of three cars with a set of two cars to realize that there are more cars altogether.

It is impossible for children to perform accurate computational activities until they are successful at object counting. Usually, they're able to add and subtract up to the number they can object count to. When counting one set, the child has to realize that to add, he needs to continue counting on from the number he had counted to.

> Leslie had a set of four butterflies. She wanted to combine those with another set of three butterflies. She counted her four butterflies, then looked at the new set and continued to count from four.

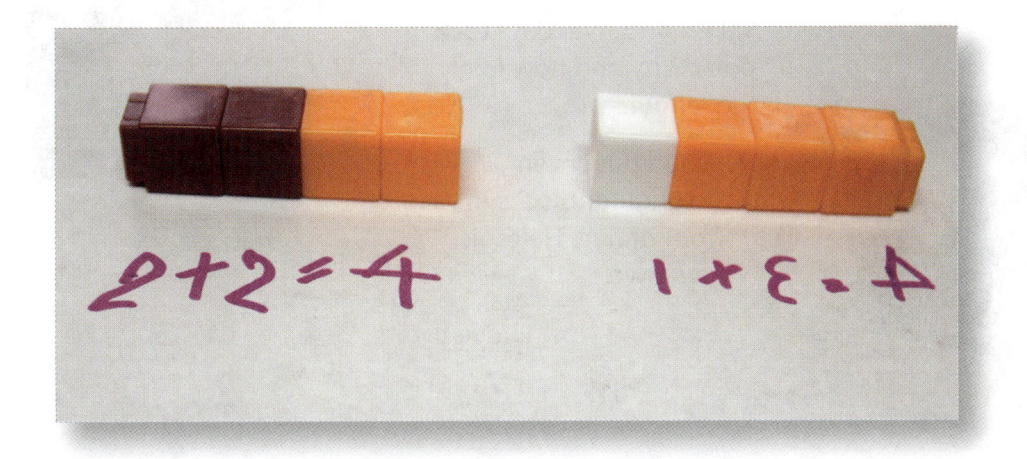

Ages and Stages of Understanding Addition and Subtraction

Children's experiences with a number of concepts depend on their abilities to engage in addition and subtraction skills. When they have had experiences with one-to-one correspondence, combining sets, object counting, and continuing to count from a known number, addition and subtraction activities begin to emerge. Their ability to add and subtract is limited by their ability to object count effectively and accurately. As a result, addition and subtraction activities tend to be within the counting range established by the child.

Chapter 10: Computation: Addition and Subtraction

Table 10.1: Ages and Stages of Understanding Addition and Subtraction

AGES	SKILLS AND ABILITIES
Three to four years old	• Counts objects to five • Adds one object to a set of up to four objects and indicates how many • Subtracts one object from a set of up to five objects and indicates how many
Four to five years old	• Counts objects to ten • Solves simple addition and subtraction problems (up to five) using concrete materials • Forms various sets of numbers that equal a specific number, depending on the child's ability to object count to that number. For example, when a child can count to eight, he forms sets of up to eight items and uses the sets formed to add or subtract items. • May begin to record number stories of sets formed

Four-year-old Bree placed five interlocking cubes in front of her. She took one away.

>   **Bree:** I had five, but I took one away and now I only have four.

Joshua put seven rectangular blocks in front of him. He took two away.

>   **Joshua:** Now I have five.

The Facilitator's Role

Although young children will engage in simple addition and subtraction activities, they will need concrete materials to manipulate to solve problems. They need to engage in active play without pressure to perform memorization tasks. As a facilitator of their learning, understand that they need to build visual representations of what addition and subtraction concepts look like. They will need to work through problems in different ways and in different settings before they can begin to transfer skills learned from one activity to another activity, and they will demonstrate their understanding in individual ways.

As in other areas, the role of the facilitator is to provide the language concepts that support addition and subtraction development. Model and reinforce the terms such as *equal to*, *take away*, *subtract*, *add to*, and *all together*.

Later, when children are ready to match and recognize number symbols, you could introduce the symbols for plus, minus, and equals, as well as number stories in the correct order such as 1 + 1 = 2.

Your observations of the children's activities are so important. Take advantage of teachable moments when you can model language and facilitate interactions.

> Annabelle, a four-year-old, was creating different sets. "Look!" Annabelle exclaimed. "Two plus three equals five!" She tried to write her number story: 2 3 5. Her teacher, Miss Jennifer, showed her how to write it using the symbols 2 + 3 = 5. Annabelle created five more number stories, and wrote them all down. Jennifer created a number book for her to use. Almost daily, Annabelle created number stories in her book using concrete materials. Eventually she proudly showed that she did not always need to use concrete materials. She could remember some of the facts.

```
5 + 2 = 7
1 + 1 = 2
2 + 2 = 4
5 + 1 = 6
```

As children build their understanding, create displays of their work, and encourage them to reflect on their learning.

Jayden: I don't need to use counters. I know all the signs, and I already know all of these.

Annabelle: I did a hard one. I made stars to help me write my number story.

Olivia: This is my number book. I work in it every day. I love adding and subtracting. So does my dad. He's a mathematician.

Ben, a six-year-old, had used the number line to solve his addition problems. He had recorded these in his math book. His teacher, Sonya, asked him how he had solved his addition problems. Ben indicated that he had used the number line. He showed how he had drawn curved lines to show his process.

SONYA: What did you learn about using a number line to solve an addition problem?

BEN: It's very easy to use, and it does not take a lot of time. You can also see the answer in your head.

SONYA: What else would you like to learn?

BEN: Well, I wonder what's on the other side of the zero.

SONYA: The numbers actually continue but are negative numbers.

Sonya showed him what that number line would look like.

BEN (very excited): Now I can subtract six from three, and the answer is negative three! See?

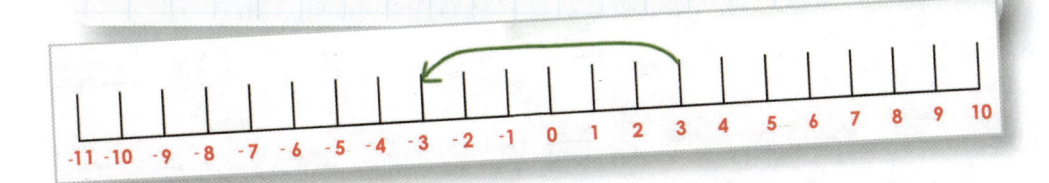

This last example clearly shows how children are thinking and that it is impossible to judge just what they are learning without asking them to reflect on their learning.

Documenting Understanding Adding and Subtracting

You can document children's learning with charts and rubrics, and the children can document their own learning.

Charts

When filling in a chart, document the dates of the observations, and briefly describe the skill you observed. Add photos, too, if you like. To say that a child has successfully mastered a skill, you will need to document at least three observations of that skill.

Sample Chart of Understanding Adding and Subtracting

Name: Jerimiah

DATES	SKILLS OBSERVED
1/10/20	Formed equal sets of 3
3/10/20	Formed two unequal sets and indicated the sum was 4
4/10/20	Added 3 plus 2 on the abacus and indicated the sum was 5

Rubrics

Sample Addition and Subtraction Rubric

Name: Annabelle

Level 1	Level 2	Level 3	Level 4
Shares objects equally using one-to-one correspondence	• Adds one object to a set of up to four objects and indicates how many • Subtracts one object from a set of up to five objects and indicates how many	Solves simple addition and subtraction problems (in sets of up to five) using concrete materials	Solves simple addition and subtraction problems (up to ten) using concrete materials and writes number stories
		1/10/20: Used abacus to add 2 + 3 = 5; wrote number story in her math book 2/10/20: Used animal counters to add 4 + 1 = 5; wrote number story in her math book 2/10/20: Counted children on climber (5) and children who jumped down (4) and indicated there was 1 person left; wrote number story in her math book	
Comments: Seems to enjoy addition and subtraction problems			

As is evident by the rubric, Annabelle has completed level 3. She is advanced for her age in computation, and therefore, the completion color is blue rather than green, indicating above-average achievement.

Children's Self-Documentation

The easiest way for children to document their own learning is to give them individual math booklets. These can be simple pages folded in half, covered with a piece of construction paper, and stapled along the folded edge. Inside, organize the pages by the level of problem solved; for example, number facts to 4. Each child can write his math stories in the booklet to show what he's learned. In addition, the children can add photographs to their pages.

Building Understanding of Addition and Subtraction

Many of the activities for addition and subtraction start with the experimentation stage for children. The greater familiarity they have with addition and subtraction concepts, the greater their understanding of these concepts. Unfortunately, much math instruction focuses on asking children to memorize facts. This type of strategy often leads to an inability to solve problems, transfer knowledge to new situations, understand the concepts of addition and subtraction, and use this information effectively. Consequently, children can develop negative feelings toward math.

In contrast, according to Mayer (2002), meaningful or conceptual learning includes understanding. Meaningful learning also leads to the ability to use prior knowledge and to transfer this knowledge to new situations. Through concrete experiences, children build the cognitive processes that lead to success at solving problems. The processes needed to solve addition and subtraction problems include spatial representation, sequential processing, visual learning, the ability to develop a plan for solving problems, problem solving, and a positive attitude toward math.

Alexander had been solving an addition problem by using counters, drawings, and a number line. He was able to represent a number problem by placing groups of objects together: a group of three rabbits and a group of four rabbits. Next, he drew two sets of ovals in his math booklet to visually represent the two groups of rabbits. He used a number line to represent the objects in each group. Then, he wrote the number story: 3 + 4 = 7. Alexander was very proud of his accomplishments. He told his mother when she came to pick him up that he was "really good at math."

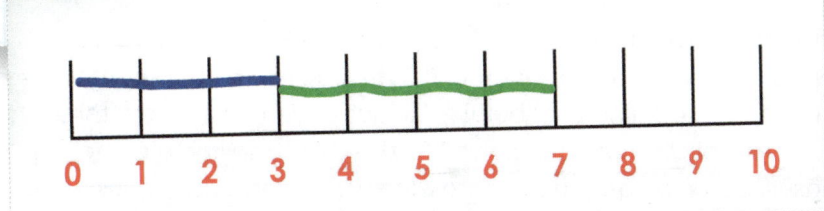

As you can see in this example, Alexander used spatial representation to express the groups of objects. When he counted his objects, he was able to use the correct sequence of numbers and to use the sequence in writing his number story. Alexander visualized how to solve his addition problem and then implemented his plans. He solved his addition problem in a number of ways: physically grouping the objects, drawing ovals to represent the objects, and using a number line. He placed counters (three rabbits and four rabbits) and drawings (three ovals and four ovals) in number arrangements, used a number line, and used symbols to represent the solution to his problem. With this success, his confidence grew.

Chapter 10: Computation: Addition and Subtraction

Activities to Build Understanding of Addition and Subtraction

Provide opportunities for free exploration to build understanding and strong foundations that will allow children to apply and transfer math concepts in various ways and settings. We have covered free-exploration activities in previous chapters: one-to-one correspondence, forming sets, object counting, and patterning. If children have had a variety of experiences in these areas, they have the foundation needed to develop addition and subtraction skills.

Equal and Unequal Sets

Provide two mats per child and a variety of counting materials, such as toy animals, toy vehicles, clothespins in a variety of colors, buttons of different sizes and colors, toy people, natural materials, geometric shapes in a variety of sizes and colors, large unit blocks, small colored unit blocks, and counters.

As children work with equal and unequal sets, ask questions such as, "How many do you have altogether?" When a child responds, rephrase his answer by modeling vocabulary: "So, when you add two to three, you get five. Two plus three equals five." As the child's ability to object count increases, accommodate his progression with appropriate questioning and modeling.

> **BRENNAN (pointing):** See? I have three on here and two here. They're not the same.
>
> **Ms. OLIVIA:** So, how many do you have altogether?
>
> **BRENNAN:** I have five.
>
> **Ms. OLIVIA:** So, three plus two equals five.

Jeremy had put out four birds on a mat. He moved two to another mat.

Jeremy: Two flew way.

Ms. Olivia: So four take away two equals two.

At snack time, Ms. Olivia observed Mark and Lamont setting a table.

Ms. Olivia: You put out four plates and four napkins. How many things did you put out altogether?

Lamont: Well, we put four and four, so (counting) eight. We have eight.

A group of children explored forming sets with the idea of creating one more or one fewer.

Cameron: First, I made nine blue shapes. Then I added one green one. Now I have ten.

Hillarie (pointing): Here are five animals. I put one more over here, so there's six animals here.

Jon, their teacher, asked Ibrahim what he had done.

Ibrahim: I put five people in a row. Then I took one away.

Jon: How many do you have now?

Ibrahim (counting): Four.

Jon: So, if you take one away from five, you get—

Ibrahim (interrupting): Four!

Application and Transfer of Concepts in Various Ways and Settings

Children need a lot of practice to form the visual memory of addition and subtraction facts in fun and realistic ways. At this stage, they'll start to solve problems in different ways, such as the following:

- Manipulating real objects to count: Two birds plus one bird equals three birds
- Creating diagrams or drawings and then writing the number story: drawing three circles and adding two circles to make five circles
- Engaging in fun, realistic activities such as creating and counting silhouettes of themselves outdoors and adding or subtracting one silhouette

Lining Up

Materials

Children

What to Do

As they line up to go outside, count the number of children in the line.

As one more child joins the line, recount: "First we had three. Now one more person came, so now we have . . ." Allow the children to count and answer.

Cleaning Up

Materials

Any materials

What to Do

Ask the children how many of a particular material they are cleaning up.

For example, if the children are cleaning up the block center, ask how many blocks they are carrying. Then, ask many they have altogether.

Learning in Action

> **Jason:** I have three blocks.
>
> **Melanie:** I am carrying four blocks.
>
> **Jason and Melanie (counting together):** One, two, three, four, five, six, seven!

Telling Number Stories

Materials

Photographs or pictures

What to Do

Children and adults take can take turns telling number stories based on photographs or pictures. These types of activities have the added advantage of encouraging children to engage in planning their activities and gathering the required resources.

Learning in Action

If you show the children a picture of animals, they may create a story like the following.

Ms. Olivia: On my way to school this morning, I saw some geese and goslings in the river. I stopped and took a picture. How many geese are there?

Joshua (counting): There are two geese and seven goslings.

Ms. Olivia: How may are there altogether?

Joshua: There's nine.

Ms. Olivia (covering two goslings with a piece of paper): Guess what: Two goslings swam away. How many goslings do we have left?

Joshua: Five.

Ms. Olivia: How many are there altogether?

Joshua: There's five goslings and two geese, so . . . seven.

Ms. Olivia showed the children a photo of toy farm animals.

Ms. Olivia: All the farm animals were together. They were talking to each other. Who would like to count them?

Jamie: There's seven.

Ms. Olivia: Well, the animals decided to go for a swim, so they all went to the pond. But the two pigs decided to play in the mud, and the sheep decided to eat the grass. So how many went in the water to swim?

Jamie: Um. (counting) Four.

Math Storyboards

Materials

Photos of scenes, such as a landscape, a woodland, a desert, a back yard, a city park, or a beach

Photographs or pictures of a number of objects, people, animals, or imaginary items

Clear contact paper or laminator

Additional objects, such as toy people or animals

Poster board

White board

Dry-erase markers

Children's math booklets

What to Do

Take or find photographs of scenes: a landscape, a woodland, a desert, a back yard, a city park, a beach, or any other scene. Cover the photos with clear contact paper or laminate for durability.

Take or find photographs or pictures of a number of objects, people, animals, or imaginary items. Cover them with clear contact paper or laminate for durability.

Set out the images, along with extra toys and figures, on a table. Place a piece of poster board on the table. Invite the children to create math storyboards.

Let a child choose a scene to place on the poster board. Invite the children to tell a story about the picture, placing images of objects, people, animals, and so on the scene.

Then, they can either add newcomers to the story by placing additional pieces on the board or draw an X on the photos of those that have left.

Next, invite them to write the number story on a white board or in their personal math booklets.

Using Number Lines

Materials

Laminated number lines

Dry-erase markers

What to Do

Children approach tasks differently when using a number line. Some children will color in the spaces, some will draw a line across the spaces, and others will make a looped line between the numbers.

Invite the children to use a number line to show a math story, such as 4 + 2 or 5 - 3.

Encourage them to write their math stories in their personal math booklets.

Learning in Action

Ben, Naomi, and Phoenix used number lines to add 4 + 2. Each used different colored markers to add the numbers 4 and 2. However, Ben colored in the spaces, Naomi drew straight lines, and Phoenix drew curved lines above the numbers. In all cases, the children arrived at the same answer and the strategy they used was visible.

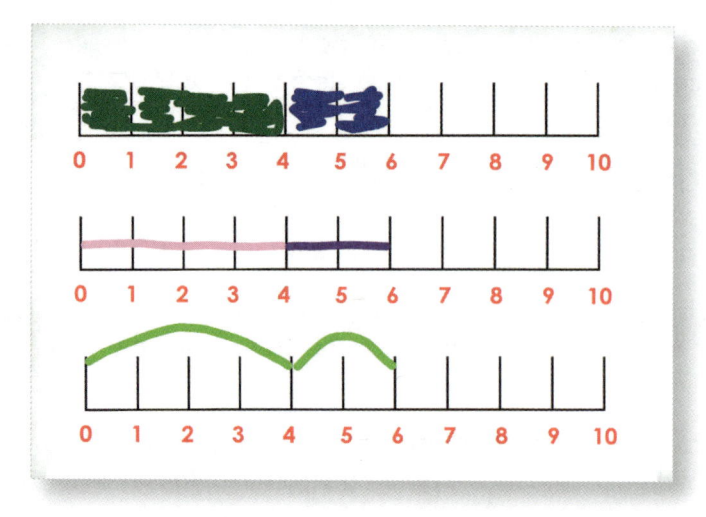

Manipulative Math Stories

Materials

Cuisenaire rods

Unit cubes

Small cubes

What to Do

Cuisenaire rods come in units of 1 to 10 so it is easy to see the relationship within numbers. They are ideal for children to use not only to form sets but also to begin to understand that numbers can be represented in different ways. Encourage the children to form sets of the same number in different ways using the different materials.

Encourage the children to write their math stories in their personal math booklets.

Learning in Action

In Malaika's preschool program, the children were excited about demonstrating their abilities to add and subtract. Jordan, Marcia, Job, and Annie used the size-five rods to create different number stories of five. Malaika then asked them what their number stories were. In each child's math booklet, she wrote their responses under their representation of the number stories. Then, she took a photograph of each child's work and placed it in each of their booklets.

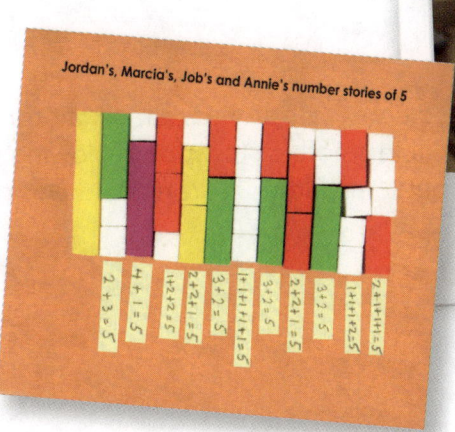

Chapter 10: Computation: Addition and Subtraction

Abacus Math Stories

Materials

Abacus

What to Do

Children also like to use an abacus. Encourage them to represent different number stories on the abacus, such as 3 + 5 = 8.

Encourage them to write their math stories in their personal math booklets.

Learning in Action

Sarah was particularly keen to use the abacus to write her number stories. She commented, "This is so easy. I love the way you can see the numbers you added. You can also take things away. You just take five or some other number and move the beads over to the side. Then you can take some away. So, five take four away just leaves one."

Light Table Math Stories

Materials

Light table

Any objects for light table

Natural objects

What to Do

Invite the children to create math stories at the light table. For example, during the fall, they could create a story about blowing leaves: "The tree still has five leaves, but three blew off. It's eight leaves altogether. The tree is almost bare."

Encourage them to write their math stories in their personal math booklets.

Block Math Stories

Materials

Blocks

Light table

Blocks and shapes for the light table

What to Do

Invite the children to create structures, either on the light table or in the block center.

Ask questions about how many blocks they are using. For example, Gia said, "I made two buildings. One has two shapes, and one has three shapes. The taller one has one more shape. It's five shapes that I used."

Encourage them to write their math stories in their personal math booklets.

Tree Math Stories

Materials

Felt, foam, or cardboard

Scissors

Containers

Card stock or index cards

Marker

What to Do

Cut bare tree shapes out of felt, foam, or cardboard. Make one for each player.

Cut leaf shapes out of felt, foam, or cardboard. Put twenty leaves in a container. Make one container of leaves for each player.

Make two decks of cards. On each card, write a number story, such as 4 + 3 or 5 - 2. Make one deck with addition number stories and one with subtraction stories.

Give each child one tree and a container of leaves. Put the addition deck in the middle of the table.

Invite the children to take turns drawing an addition card. They then solve the addition problem by putting the required number of leaves on their tree and saying the total number of leaves.

When all the cards are gone, they can start with the subtraction cards. They take off the number of leaves to solve the problem. They can play until a player has no more leaves left.

Nature Math Stories

Materials

Natural items, such as small sticks, rocks, shells, pine cones, acorns, leaves, or seeds

Containers

Labels

Card stock or index cards

Large pieces of card stock

Markers

What to Do

On a field trip outdoors, invite the children to collect natural items such as pine cones, leaves, shells, acorns, seeds or small stones.

Back inside, encourage the children to sort the items into categories and then put them into containers. Let them label the containers by picture and word. Help as needed.

They can then use one or more containers to form addition number stories. They can use the same cards used for the Tree Math Stories game, or you can make new sets for this game. Place the cards in the middle of the table.

On a large piece of card stock, draw ten squares and write the numbers 1 to 10 in the squares, one number per square. Make a number grid for each player.

To play, a child draws an addition card. He then selects objects to express that number story and puts the items in the square with the number that represents the total.

If a child draws a card with a total that is already filled on his card, the next player takes a turn. Once the children have used up all the items or one of the children has filled all of his squares, they all switch to the subtraction cards.

The game ends when none of the subtraction cards can be used. The player with the least number of filled squares wins.

Learning in Action

A group of children played using stones, acorns, and leaves. Jeremy turned up the card that had 2 + 3 written on it. He chose two stones and three acorns and placed the items in the square numbered 5.

Later in the game, Jeremy turned up the card that said 9 - 7. He looked on his card and saw that he had nine items in the 9 square. He then took seven away. He moved those items to the 2 square.

Math Games

Children will build their understanding of adding and subtracting as they play games that involve adding scores or adding the number of dots on a pair of dice. Games that use dice, such as Tenzi, encourage a number of concepts, including number recognition and adding the sum of two dice. In Tenzi, as children build, they add up the number of blocks needed or subtract the ones they took off.

The next time you and the children go on a field trip to collect natural items such as pine cones, small stones, shells, leaves, twigs, or seeds, try this idea. Bring the items back to the classroom, and organize them by type. Once the items are organized, the children can engage in activities such as adding all the red leaves to the green leaves, or subtracting the number of red leaves from the number of green leaves. Encourage them to see how many variations of adding and subtracting they can come up with and to write the number stories in their math booklets.

Learning in Action

Jonathan used two large foam dice to create his number stories. He rolled a six and a five. He then counted the dots on the dice and printed his number story in his math booklet: 6 + 5 = 11.

Chapter Summary

Memorizing math facts is not a strategy that leads to sustainable learning retention, because understanding is not part of the memorization process. Children need opportunities to form visualizations of what various combinations of addition and subtraction look like, explore their own unique ways of representing their understanding, develop a variety of strategies to solve addition and subtraction problems, transfer their learning from one situation to another, and reflect on what they have learned and still need to learn.

Apply the Learning

1. When would it be appropriate to encourage children to solve addition and subtraction problems? Provide a rationale for your answers.

   Reflect on how you feel about the field of mathematics. Did you or do you enjoy math as a subject? How might your feelings affect your ability to be an effective math teacher?

   What additional information or training might you need, and where could you find it?
2. Young children start simple calculations very early. Why do you think this happens?

   How can you encourage and support these early explorations? What activities might you provide to encourage children's problem-solving skills?
3. Describe what Annie has done in this photo. How would you support her learning? What other materials might you provide Annie to expand upon her learning?

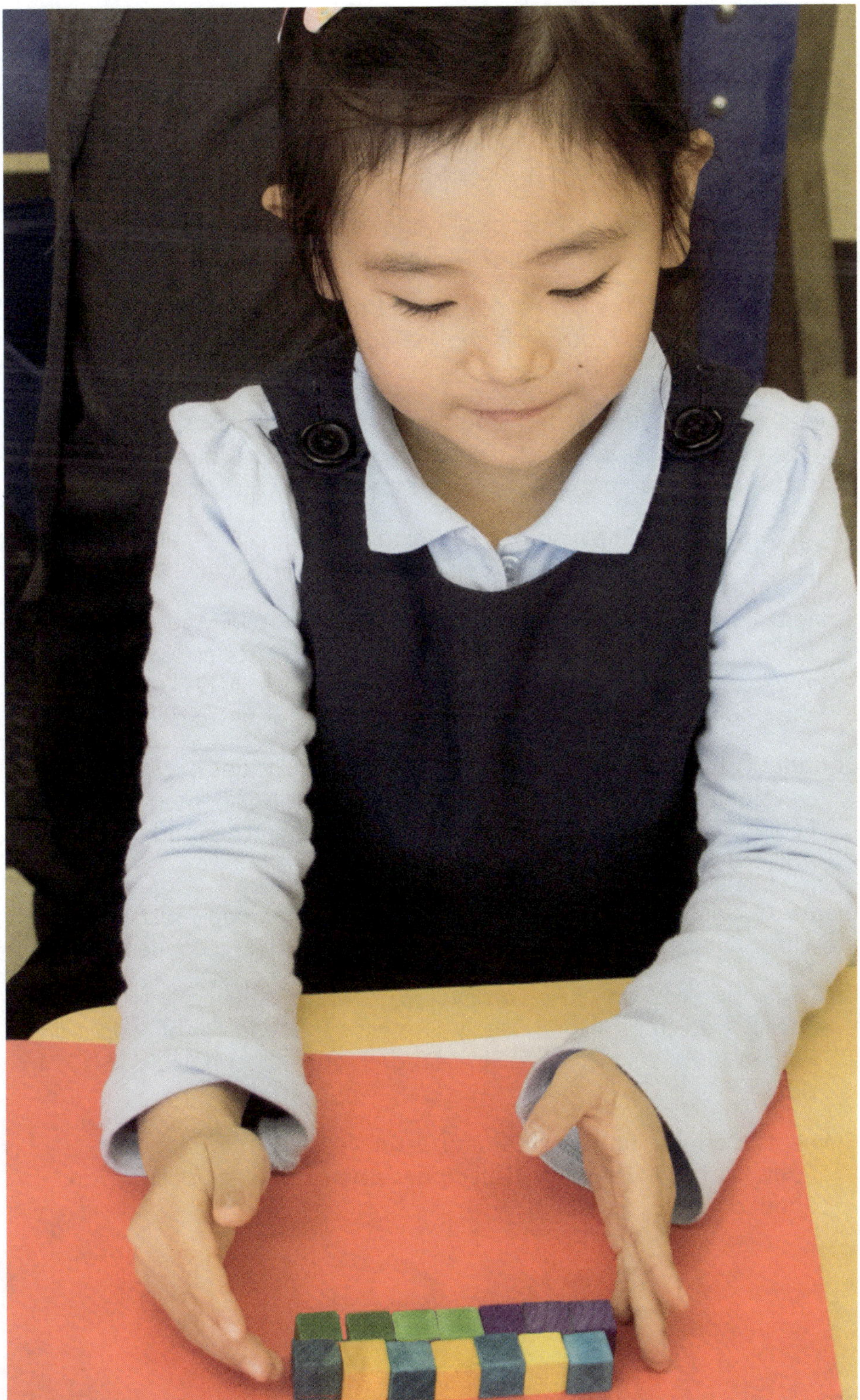

References and Recommended Reading

Alphonso, Caroline. 2018. "Falling Ontario Test Scores Add to National Math Debate." *The Globe and Mail*, August 29. https://www.theglobeandmail.com/canada/article-ontario-pushes-for-more-teacher-training-as-math-score-hits-new-low/

Barrouillet, Pierre. 2015. "Theories of Cognitive Development: From Piaget to Today." *Developmental Review* 38: 1–12.

Boaler, Jo. 2016. *Mathematical Mindsets: Unleashing Students' Potential through Creative Math, Inspiring Messages and Innovative Teaching.* San Francisco: Jossey-Bass.

Brabeck, Mary, Jill Jeffrey, and Sara Fry. 2010. "Practice for Knowledge Acquisition (Not Drill and Kill)." American Psychological Association. https://www.apa.org/education/k12/practice-acquisition

Briggs, Mary. 2013. *Teaching and Learning Early Years Mathematics: Subject and Pedagogic Knowledge.* Norwich, UK: Critical Publishing.

Camera, Lauren. 2019. "Across the Board, Scores Drop in Math and Reading for U.S. Students." *US News and World Report*, October 30. https://www.usnews.com/news/education-news/articles/2019-10-30/across-the-board-scores-drop-in-math-and-reading-for-us-students

Canadian Child Care Federation. 2009. "Ages and Stages of Numeracy Development." Resource Sheet #95. Ottawa, ON: Canadian Child Care Federation. https://www.cccf-fcsge.ca/wp-content/uploads/RS_95-e.pdf

Clements, Douglas, and Julie Sarama. 2009. *Learning and Teaching Early Math: The Learning Trajectories Approach.* New York: Routledge.

Clements, Douglas, and Julie Sarama. 2013. "Math in the Early Years: A Strong Predictor for Later School Success." *The Progress of Education Reform* 14(5): 1–7. https://www.ecs.org/clearinghouse/01/09/46/10946.pdf

Clements, Douglas, and Julie Sarama. 2014. *Learning and Teaching Early Math: The Learning. Trajectories Approach.* 2nd ed. New York: Routledge.

Clements, Douglas, and Julie Sarama. 2019. *Learning and Teaching with Learning Trajectories: Early Math Birth to Grade 3*. Denver, CO: Marsico Institute, Morgridge College of Education, University of Denver. https://www.learningtrajectories.org/documents/1571675010308.pdf

Crowther, Ingrid. 2018a. *Creating Effective Learning Environments*. Toronto, ON: Nelson Canada.

Crowther, Ingrid. 2018b. *Engaging in Reflective Thinking*. Edmonton, AB: Lifelong Learn, Inc.

Crowther, Ingrid. 2018c. *Rubric Development*. Edmonton, AB: Lifelong Learn, Inc.

Duncan, Greg J., et al. 2007. "School Readiness and Later Achievement." *Developmental Psychology* 43(6): 1428–1446.

Eckhoff, Angela. 2017. *Creative Investigations in Early Math*. Lewisville, NC: Gryphon House.

European Commission Directorate-General for Education and Culture. 2013. *Thematic Working Group on Mathematics, Science, and Technology (2010–2013) Final Report: Addressing Low Achievement in Mathematics and Science*. https://ec.europa.eu/assets/eac/education/experts-groups/2011-2013/mst/wg-mst-final-report_en.pdf

Fox, Jill Englebright, and Robert Schirrmacher. 2015. *Art and Creative Development for Young Children*. 8th ed. Stamford, CT: Cengage Learning.

Hattie, John, Douglas Fisher, and Nancy Frey. 2017. *Visible Learning for Mathematics Grades K-12: What Works Best to Optimize Student Learning*. Thousand Oaks, CA: Corwin.

Kilpatrick, Jeremy, W. Gary Martin, and Deborah Schifter. 2003. *A Research Companion to Principles and Standards for School Mathematics*. Reston, VA: National Council of Teachers of Mathematics.

King, Patricia, and Karen Strohm Kitchener. 1994. *Developing Reflective Judgment*. San Francisco: Jossey-Bass.

Mayer, Richard. 2002. "Rote versus Meaningful Learning." *Theory into Practice* 41(4): 226–232.

Montessori Academy. 2017. "Repetition and Child Development in Montessori Education." Montessori Academy. https://montessoriacademy.com.au/repetition-child-development-montessori/

National Association for the Education of Young Children and National Council of Teachers of Mathematics. 2002. "Early Childhood Mathematics: Promoting Good Beginnings." Joint Position Statement. Washington, DC: NAEYC and NCTM.

National Council of Teachers of Mathematics. 2000. *Principles and Standards for School Mathematics*. Reston, VA: NCTM.

Nunes, Terezinha, Peter Bryant, and Anne Watson. 2009. "Key Understandings in Mathematics Learning. Paper 1: Overview." London, UK: Nuffield Foundation. https://mk0nuffieldfounpg9ee.kinstacdn.com/wp-content/uploads/2019/12/P1.pdf

Platas, Linda. 2018. "Measuring Up! Measurement in the Preschool Classroom." Development and Research in Early Math Education. https://dreme.stanford.edu/news/measuring-measurement-preschool-classroom

Reid, Kate, and Nicole Andrews. 2016. *Fostering Understanding of Early Numeracy Development*. Camberwell, Vic: Australian Council for Educational Research. https://research.acer.edu.au/cgi/viewcontent.cgi?article=1028&context=monitoring_learning

Research and Development Institute. 2006. "One-to-One Correspondence and Counting Skills." Project Math Access. http://www.tsbvi.edu/mathproject/ch1-sec3.asp

Robertson, Juliet. 2017. *Messy Maths: A Playful, Outdoor Approach for Early Years*. Carmarthen, Wales, UK: Independent Thinking Press.

Shumway, Jessica. 2011. *Number Sense Routines: Building Numerical Literacy Every Day in Grades K–3*. Portland, NH: Stenhouse.

Small, Marian. 2017. *Making Math Meaningful for Canadian Students K–8*. 3rd ed. Toronto, ON: Nelson Education.

Tarrant, Kate. 2014. *Assessment: Effective Use of Appropriate Assessments in Prekindergarten through 3rd Grade: Building a Strong Foundation for the Common Core Learning Standards*. Rensselaer, NY: State Early Childhood Advisory Council. http://nysaeyc.org/wp-content/uploads/DAP-AssessmentSixPageWeb.pdf

Index

A

Abacus math stories, 266
Absorption, 75-76
Academic success
   math as a predictor of, 6-8
Active learning, 26
Activities
   addition and subtraction, 258-270
   conservation, 132-135
   forming sets, 88-93, 98-100
   geometrical shapes, 213-224
   measurement, 185-198
   object counting, 117, 121-135
   one-to-one correspondence, 47-76
   parts and wholes, 234-244
   patterning, 158-172
Addition and subtraction, 246-270
   activities, 258-270
   ages and stages, 249-250
   application and transfer of concepts, 260-269
   building understanding, 256-257
   documenting learning, 254-256
   facilitator's role, 251-253
   games, 269-270
Ages and stages
   addition and subtraction, 249-250
   forming sets, 81
   geometrical shapes, 203
   measurement skills, 178
   object counting, 105-106
   one-to-one correspondence, 43-44
   parts and wholes, 229

   patterning, 149-150
   puzzles, 63
Alignment, 80
Application and transfer of concepts, 260-269
   abacus math stories, 266
   block math stories, 267
   cleaning up, 260-271
   light table math stories, 266-267
   lining up, 260
   manipulative math stories, 265
   math storyboards, 263
   nature math stories, 268-269
   telling number stories, 261-262
   tree math stories, 267-268
   using number lines, 264
Area, 95, 179, 188-189, 198
Arrival and departure routines, 48
Art center
   draw a set, 122
   math and, 7
   measurement skills, 191
   object counting, 121-122
   one-to-one correspondence, 55-58
   painting, drawing, and printmaking, 56-57
   parts and wholes, 234-235
   print patterns, 163
   printmaking, 121
   sculpting and collage, 57-58
   unequal parts, 234-235
   weaving, 191
Assessment
   formative, 34, 36-37, 39
   of math abilities, 33-35
   summative, 34

Associative play, 21, 23
Attributes
    geometrical shapes, 202
    measurement skills, 178
    patterns, 148, 158-160

B

Baby care
    one-to-one correspondence, 59-60
Balancing, 49, 76
Ball skills, 50
Bilateral symmetry, 168
Block play
    build a farm, 53-54
    building with parts and wholes, 236
    challenge cards, 123
    forming sets, 97
    math stories, 267
    measuring structures, 192
    object counting, 122-123
    one-to-one correspondence, 53-54
    patterning, 164
Booklets, 230-231
Build a farm, 53-54
Building activities into routines
    arrival and departure, 48
    one-to-one correspondence, 47-50
    outdoor free play, 49-50
    snack and meal times, 47-48
    transitions, 48-49
Building understanding
    forming sets, 84-85
    geometrical shapes, 211-217
    incorporating object counting, 145
    measurement skills, 183-184
    number recognition, 115-117
    number sequencing, 113-114
    object counting, 118-120
    ordinals, 114-115
    parts and wholes, 233-234
    patterning, 156-172
    recognition of common shapes, 218-220

C

Carpentry area
    materials and activities, 70-71
    measuring skills, 193-194
    oject counting, 124
    one-to-one correspondence, 68-71
    precarpentry skills, 69
Centration, 11
Challenge cards
    forming sets, 98-99
    object counting, 123
    shapes, 214-215, 223-224
Charts. *See* Skill charts
Checklists
    defined, 36
    developmental, 36
    geometrical shapes, 205
    object counting, 109, 111
    samples, 111
Children's books
    about measurement, 192
    about object counting, 125, 144-145
    about one-to-one correspondence, 55
    about parts and wholes, 237
    about patterning, 165, 172-173
    about shapes, 218

Children's thinking, 8-18
- egocentric, 9
- reflective, 13-18, 22
- symbolic, 10-13

Choices, 26, 32
- forming sets, 84, 90-93
- geometric shapes, 225
- object counting, 119

Circumference, 179, 187
Clean up, 260-261
Colors
- absorption, 75-76
- forming sets, 97
- measurement skills, 195-196
- mixing, 74-75
- one-to-one correspondence, 64, 74-76

Comparing
- forming sets, 99-100
- geometrical shapes, 211-212
- language, 179, 194
- measurement, 176, 178
- sizes, 133

Comparison sets
- challenge cards, 98-99
- lily pad comparisons, 99-100
- planning for, 94-100

Computation.
  Addition and Subtraction
Conceptual learning, 256-257
Conservation, 35
- activities, 132-135
- comparing sizes, 133
- counting sets, 134-135
- it's the same number, 134
- object counting, 103, 106, 132
- of measurement, 176
- of number, 132-135
- one-to-one squares, 133

Constructing shapes, 220-221
Construction toys, 61-62
Convergent thinking, 7
Cooking
- measurement skills, 197-198
- ordinals, 115
- parts and wholes, 243-244
- playdough, 197

Cooperative play, 22
Counter match, 127-128
Cube collector, 127

D

Developing math concepts, 4-22
- how children's thinking affects, 8-18, 22
- how fine-motor control affects learning, 18-19, 22
- how play affects, 19-22

Developmental checklists, 36
Diameter, 188
Direct instruction vs. facilitated instruction, 31-32
Distance, 179, 196
Divergent thinking, 7
Documentating learning, 8
- addition and substraction, 254-256
- booklets, 230-231
- checklists, 111, 205
- formative strategies, 36-37, 39
- forming sets, 81-83
- geometrical shapes, 204-210
- graphs, 110-111, 151-153, 181, 208-210
- individual number books, 109
- math abilities, 33-35
- measurement skills, 181-182
- object counting, 109-112

Index

one-to-one correspondence, 44-46, 77
panels, 151, 155, 173
parts and wholes, 230-232
patterning, 151-155, 173
photographic evidence, 45
rubric development, 46
rubrics, 81-83, 112, 151, 153-154, 182, 207, 231-232, 255-256
self-documentation, 256
skill charts, 44-45, 81-82, 151-152, 182, 206, 254

Dramatic play
baby care, 59-60
kitchen, 60-61
object counting, 124
one-to-one correspondence, 58-61
pattern dress-up, 164

E

Egocentric thinking, 9
Equal and unequal, 87, 94-97, 100
    challenge cards, 98-99
    object counting, 103
    sets, 258-259
Estimating, 176
Eye-hand coordination, 18, 68-71, 197-198, 243-244

F

Facilitated instruction, 31-32, 37-38
Facilitator's role, 2, 24-39
    addition and subtraction, 251-253
    choosing materials, 28-29
    direct vs. facilitated instruction, 31-32
    documenting and assessing math abilities, 33-35
    facilitating learning, 37-38
    formative documentation strategies, 36-37
    forming sets, 87-88
    geometrical shapes, 203-204
    measurement skills, 179
    object counting, 106-108
    organizing materials, 29-30
    organizing workspaces and displays, 30-31
    parts and wholes, 229-230
    patterning, 151
    planning, 33
    providing guidance and support, 31-39
    providing organized spaces, 26-31

Families
    arrival and departure, 48
    forming sets, 96, 100
    geometric shapes, 210, 225
    interacting with, 2
    object counting, 132, 145

Field trips
    finding patterns in nature, 155, 168-173
    geometric shapes, 224-225
    nature math stories, 268-269
    object counting, 132

Find-a-shape mats, 215-216

Fine-motor control
    affects math learning, 18-19, 22
    carpentry, 68-71
    cutting fruit, 243-244
    measuring skills, 197-198

Formative assessment, 36-37, 39

Forming sets, 78-100
   addition and subtraction, 249-250, 258
   ages and stages, 81
   building understanding, 84-86
   documenting, 81-83
   facilitator's role, 87-88
   object counting, 103
   planning for comparison sets, 94-100
   planning introductory activities, 88-93
Fractals, 168-169
Frustration, 37-38

G

Games, 217-218, 269-270
Geometric shapes, 200-225
   activities, 213-224
   ages and stages, 203
   books about, 218
   building recognition, 218-220
   building understanding, 211-212
   constructing, 220-221
   documenting learning, 204-210
   facilitator's role, 203-204
   identifying components, 221-224
   materials, 211-212
   parts and wholes, 228
   patterns, 162
   tangram counting, 129-130
Graphs
   geometrical shapes, 208-210
   measurement skills, 181
   object counting, 109-110
   patterning, 151-152

H

Height, 183-185, 192, 198

I

Identifying components of shapes, 221-224
Individual number books, 109
Intentional learning approach, 28, 158

L

Language development, 1-2
   addition and subtraction, 251
   comparitive, 179, 194
   equal/not equal, 94-97, 100, 103
   geometrical shapes, 202-204
   math and, 7
   measurement, 176, 179, 191
   more than/less than, 87, 95, 100, 103
   number words, 115
   one-to-one correspondence, 51
   parts and wholes, 228-229, 244
   patterning, 151
   positional words, 51, 63-67, 69-70
   sequencing, 114
Learning centers
   art, 7, 55-58, 121-122, 163, 191, 234-235
   block, 53-54, 97, 122-123, 164, 192, 236, 267
   carpentry, 68-72, 124, 193-194
   dramatic play, 58-61, 124, 164
   forming sets, 97
   library, 55, 125, 165, 192
   manipulatives, 18, 26, 61-67, 84, 166, 194, 211-212, 238, 260, 265

outdoors, 49-50, 100, 126, 131, 145, 149, 156-157, 168-172, 195, 243, 268-269
puzzles and games area, 51-53, 61-63, 239-241
sand and water, 166, 241-252
science, 8, 71-76, 125, 167, 194-198
Length, 186, 193-195, 198
Library center, 125, 165, 192
Light table math stories, 266-267
Lily pad comparisons, 99-100
Line patterns, 158, 161-162

M

Manipulating objects, 18, 26
  addition and subtraction, 260, 265
  geometrical shapes, 211-212
Manipulatives area
  forming sets, 84
  measure and compare, 194
  one-to-one correspondence, 61-67
  parts and wholes, 238
  patterning, 166
  puzzles by age and stage, 63
  ways to make five, 238
Matching skills
  butterflies, 51-53
  by size, 97
  geometrical shapes, 211-214
  math and, 7-8
  numbers, 116
  object counting, 126-129
  parts and wholes, 239
Materials
  choosing, 28-29, 39
  forming sets, 86, 100
  geometrical shapes, 211-212
  organizing, 29-30, 86, 100, 244
  patterning, 158-162
Math stories
  abacus, 266
  block, 267
  light table, 266-267
  manipulative, 265
  nature, 268-269
  number, 261-262
  tree, 267-268
Math storyboards, 263
Meaningful learning, 256-257
Measurement skills, 17, 174-198
  activities for, 185-198
  ages and stages, 178
  area, 179, 188-189, 198
  art center, 191
  block center, 193
  building understanding of, 183-184
  carpentry, 193-194
  circumference, 179, 187
  diameter, 188
  distance, 179, 196
  documenting learning, 181-182
  facilitator's role, 179-181
  height, 183-185, 193-194, 198
  language, 176, 179
  length, 186, 193-195, 198
  library center, 192
  making playdough, 197-198
  manipulatives, 194
  outdoor play, 195
  perimeter, 179-180, 187, 198
  science center, 195-196
  seriation, 190
  using nonstandard tools, 176, 178

volume, 179, 189-190, 195, 198
Memory games, 217
More than/less than, 87, 94-95, 100
    challenge cards, 98-99
    object counting, 103
Music activities, 7, 114, 135-139, 165

N

Number lines, 264
Number recognition
    building understanding, 115-117
    object counting, 103, 115-117
    roll and match the number, 117
    twisty numbers, 117
Number stories, 261-262
Numbers
    matching, 129
    patterns, 148
    sequencing, 103, 113-114, 132

O

Object counting, 8, 17, 39, 102-145
    activities, 126-130
    addition and subtraction, 248-250, 258
    ages and stages, 105-106
    art center, 121-122
    block center, 122-123
    building understanding, 118-120
    carpentry, 124
    conservation, 103, 106, 132-135
    documenting learning, 109-112
    dramatic play, 124
    facilitator's role, 107-109
    field trips, 131
    forming sets, 96, 103
    geometrical shapes, 211-212
    higher numbers equal greater
        quantities, 103
    library, 125, 144-145
    number recognition, 103, 115-117
    number sequence, 103, 113-114
    one-to-one correspondence, 43, 103
    ordinals, 103, 106, 114-115
    outdoor play, 126, 145
    rhymes to support, 141-144
    rote, 106
    science center, 125
    shape characteristics, 223
    songs to support, 135-140
    understanding terms, 103
One-to-one correspondence, 7-8, 40-77
    addition and subtraction, 249, 258
    ages and stages of, 43-44
    building activities into learning centers, 51-76
    building activities into routines, 47-50
    documenting, 44-46
    facilitator's role, 47
    forming sets, 80, 96-97, 100
    kits, 77
    object counting, 43, 103, 132-133
Ordinals, 103, 106, 114-115
Organization
    benefits of, 27
    materials, 29-30, 86, 100
    providing spaces, 26-31
    workspaces and displays, 30-31
Outdoor play
    equal sets, 243
    forming sets, 100
    measurement skills, 195
    nature math stories, 268-269

Index

object counting, 126, 131, 145
one-to-one correspondence, 49-50
parts and wholes, 243
patterning, 149, 156-157, 168-172
Overexcitement, 37

P

Painting, drawing, and printmaking
    one-to-one correspondence, 56-57
Parallel play, 20-21
Parts and wholes, 226-244
    activities, 235-244
    ages and stages, 229
    art center, 234-235
    block center, 236
    books about, 237
    building understanding, 233-234
    documenting learning, 230-232
    facilitator's role, 229-230
    geometric shapes and, 228
    manipulative, 238
    outdoor play, 243
    puzzles and games, 239-241
    sand and water center, 241-242
    snack/mealtime, 243-244
Patterning, 12, 146-175
    activities, 163-172
    addition and subtration, 258
    ages and stages, 149-150
    building understanding of, 156-158
    by attributes, 148, 150, 158-160
    centration, 11
    cooperative play, 22
    documenting, 151-155, 173
    facilitator's role, 28, 35, 151
    geometric shapes, 162
    line, 148, 161-162
    math and, 7
    number, 148
    organizing materials, 158
    resources to support, 172-173
Patterns, 7, 149, 168-172
Perimeter, 95, 179-180, 187, 198
Photographic evidence, 44-45
Place value, 18
Planning, 33
    for comparison sets, 94-97
    for number sequencing, 113-114
    introductory activities, 88-93
Play
    affects math learning, 19-22
    as learning, 39
    associative, 21
    cooperative, 22
    forming sets, 100
    one-to-one correspondence, 49-50
    outdoor, 49-50, 100
    parallel, 20-22
    solitary, 19-20
Prereflective thinking stage, 15-16
Print patterns, 163
Printmaking, 121
Problem solving
    math skills and, 6-7
    object counting, 107-108
Providing guidance and support, 31-39
    direct vs. facilitated instruction, 31-32
    documenting and assessing math abilities, 33-35

facilitating learning, 37-38
formative documentation strategies, 36-37
planning, 33
Puzzles and games area
  butterfly matching, 51-53
  by age and stage, 63
  nature fractions, 240-241
  one-to-one correspondence, 51-53, 61-63
  parts and wholes, 239-241
  picture mix and match, 239

Q
Quantitative relations, 77

R
Reflective thinking, 13-18
  addition and subtraction, 252-253
  forming sets, 85
  measurement skills, 198
  stage, 15-16
Reinforcement, 37-38
Repetition, 36
Resources
  to support counting, 135-145
  to support patterning, 172-173
Responsive listening, 38
Rhymes, 7, 114, 141-144
Rhythm, 165
Riding, 50
Roll and build, 128
Roll and match the number, 117
Rubrics, 36
  addition and subtraction, 255-256
  defined, 36

development, 44, 46
forming sets, 82-83
geometrical shapes, 207
measurement skills, 182
object counting, 109, 112
one-to-one correspndence, 46
parts and wholes, 231-232
patterning, 151, 153-154

S
Sand and water center
  parts and wholes, 241-242
  patterning, 166
  seriation cups, 242
Scaffolding, 37
Science area
  balance, 76
  color absorption, 75-76
  color mixing, 74-75
  creating mixtures, 194-196
  drip patterns, 167
  magnetic patterns, 167
  making playdough, 197-198
  math and, 8
  measuring distance, 196
  object counting, 125
  one-to-one correspondence, 71-76
  sink or float, 72
  solutions, 74
  suspensions, 73
Sculpting and collage, 57-58
Self-criticism, 23
Self-documentation, 256
Seriation, 190, 242
Sink or float, 72
Size
  comparing, 133

forming sets, 80
Skill charts, 44-45
   addition and subtraction, 254
   forming sets, 81-82
   geometrical shapes, 206, 215
   measurement skills, 182
   object counting, 111
   one-to-one correspondence, 44-45
   patterning, 151-152
Snack and mealtimes
   cutting fruit, 243-244
   one-to-one correspondence, 47-48
   parts and wholes, 243-244
Solitary play, 19-20
Solutions, 74
Songs, 7, 114, 135-140
Sorting skills
   forming sets, 80
   geometrical shapes, 213-214
   math and, 7-8
Spatial awareness/relationships
   addition and subtraction, 257
   forming sets, 95
   geometric shapes, 202
   math and, 7
   one-to-one correspondence, 77
   patterning, 148
Spirals, 168-169
Spontaneous teaching opportunities, 107, 109, 113-114, 173
Spots and stripes, 168-169
Stress, 37
Subtraction. *See* Addition and subtraction
Summative assessment, 34

Suspensions, 73
Symbolic thinking, 10-13
Symmetry, 168-169

T
Tangram counting, 129-130
Transitions, 48-49
Tree math stories, 267-268
Tripod grasp, 18-19
Twisty numbers, 117

V
Volume, 179, 189-190, 195-196, 198

W
Weight, 189, 198
Writing skills, 7